THE COMPLETE GUIDE
TO
WHEAT-FREE COOKING

THE COMPLETE GUIDE
TO
WHEAT-FREE
COOKING

Phyllis Potts

Foreword by
John A. Green, M.D.

BEYOND
WORDS
Publishing
I N C

Beyond Words Publishing, Inc.
20827 N.W. Cornell Road, Suite 500
Hillsboro, Oregon 97124-9808
503-531-8700
1-800-284-9673

Editor: Sue Mann
Proofreader: Hilary Russell
Cover design: Bill Stanton
Typographer: Pamela Martin
Managing editor: Kathy Matthews

Printed in Malaysia
Distributed to the book trade by Publishers Group West

Library of Congress Cataloging-in-Publication Data
Potts, Phyllis L.
    The complete guide to wheat-free cooking / Phyllis Potts.
      p. cm.
    Includes index.
    ISBN 1-885223-77-3 (paperback)
    1. Wheat-free diet—Recipes.   I. Title.
RM237.87.P679   1998
641.5′63—dc21   97-51320
                                       CIP

The corporate mission of Beyond Words Publishing, Inc.:
Inspire to Integrity

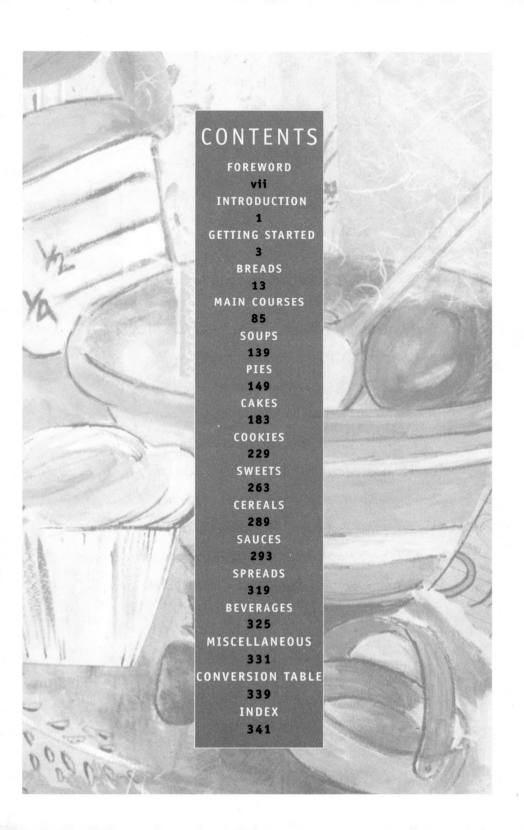

CONTENTS

From the treasure box . . .

I wish to acknowledge . . .

Husband, Ed, for his tasting and his support.
Children, Natalie, Harvey, and Neal for their
encouragement.
Dick Lutz for being my mentor.
Emily Orlando, instructor, editor, and friend.
Sue Mann for her editorial expertise.
Kathy Matthews for her patience.
Dr. John A. Green, M.D. for his suggestions.
Beyond Words Publishing, Inc. for taking on this project.
Everyone who tasted and said, "Put it in the book!"

FOREWORD

If I can stop one Heart from breaking
I shall not live in vain.
If I can ease one Life the Aching
Or cool one Pain

Or help one fainting Robin
Unto his Nest again
I shall not live in Vain.
—Emily Dickinson

Ten years ago a woman came into my practice for evaluation of a list of chronic health problems. The list, though a bit long and daunting, was common to a number of patients I had been successful at helping. We set about exploring her physiology, looking for explanations in various digestive studies, allergy tests, and hormone tests, without really succeeding. I did not see her for quite some time, and then she came in to tell me about her progress and to share a wheat-free delight she had made. She had found relief in avoiding wheat and had also started collecting helpful and delicious recipes.

Every so often she would come in to update me about her condition and share another delicious example of her wheat-free recipes. I enjoyed her visits as much for the treats she brought as for the progress she reported. Then Phyllis (you already guessed her name, didn't you) called one day and asked if I would write a foreword to her book on cooking without wheat. I agreed to do so as long as I could have a copy; I had

found at about the same time as she that wheat and I do not get along well together.

In this book Phyllis has done what only exceptional people do; face their illnesses and let them be teachers. Her readers are gifted by Phyllis's illness in that it has taught her how to teach us to go beyond just coping or surviving. In this book she shows us how to thrive, even delight in following a wheat-free diet. With a five-year-old daughter who is also wheat sensitive, I have had the opportunity to serve birthday parties to discriminating children, Thanksgiving feasts to even more discriminating adults, and even cook wheat free on backpacking trips, all without a single failure.

Try some of these recipes, even if you are not wheat sensitive. You will enjoy them and probably improve your nutrition significantly. For example, the garbanzo flour is an excellent source of magnesium and fiber, two nutrients commonly deficient in our diet.

If you have some sort of undiagnosed health problem, such as chronic headaches, respiratory ailments, chronic joint and muscle pains, chronic intestinal disturbances, or stubborn skin problems, try a wheat-avoidance diet. You may be gratified as many of my patients and I have been. I wish you good eating and good health.

—John Green, M.D.

INTRODUCTION

One of the most exciting days of my life was when the Cable News Network came to my home! CNN was interested in knowing more about people who were sensitive to wheat and that I was publishing *Going Against the Grain Wheat-Free Cookery* by myself on the dining room table! Caroline O'Neil from "On the Menu" was here for three hours. "Thank goodness you're here," I said. "Now I can stop cleaning!" The resulting avalanche of calls from all over the United States, Canada, New Zealand, and the Virgin Islands was totally unexpected. And time after time people asked me for bread, pizza, and pie crust recipes.

Many people who called or wrote were gluten intolerant, and they were grateful for my combination of rice and bean flours because it is a combination that they could safely use. However, because I am not gluten intolerant, I included a few recipes using grains other than wheat that should be avoided by the gluten intolerant.

MY PURPOSE

Those of us who are aware of the foods we must avoid to feel well unfortunately tend to focus on the negative rather than on the positive. Eating becomes a chore when the list of negative foods becomes a long one. It is downright depressing to be told that we have to cut out bread, hamburger rolls, hot dogs, pancakes, pies, cookies, cakes, pizza—everything we ever enjoyed

eating. And every social occasion includes eating. We are invited to teas, desserts, potlucks, happy hours, weddings, and funerals—all serving wonderful things we cannot eat.

> **Eating is not merely a material pleasure. Eating well gives a spectacular joy to life and contributes immensely to goodwill and happy companionship. It is of great importance to the morale.**
> —Elsa Schiaparelli, *Shocking Life*

Most of us need to discover and work with our food sensitivities. Allergy specialist Dr. John A. Green of Aurora, Oregon, encourages people who don't know why they feel ill to try wheat- and dairy-free recipes for a few weeks to see if avoiding these foods makes a difference. Therefore, my purpose is to present truly delicious wheat-free recipes in a manner that sparks enthusiasm for cooking and eating. This book makes good eating attainable for those who must change their eating habits. It is easier on the cook, who is trying to keep everyone happy, by eliminating the need for separate foods for other family members. I believe everyone will enjoy these wheat-free recipes!

GETTING STARTED

ABOUT THE RECIPES . . .

Longing for good food is what has prompted me to choose recipes for their "country good" background. These are the older, treasured family recipes that have been modified to accommodate those who cannot eat wheat. Although I have looked for dairy- and egg-free recipes also, I do use these ingredients in a few recipes, but I usually provide some options.

Many of us are working people who have so little time, it seems, for cooking. How do we cope with all the extra cooking needed for special diets? I provide suggestions for making the cook's job more efficient. I emphasize simple recipes, although a few require more time. They are so special and so good that you may want to consider them for special occasions. There are recipes for mixes that can be stored or frozen, thus cutting down on preparation time. There are new recipes, because I keep discovering more ways to replace old favorites.

ABOUT EQUIPMENT . . .

- Bread machines do make wheat-free breads, but you will need to make adjustments to your recipes. See more information about bread machines in the BREADS chapter. The pluses for a bread machine are that it is a great time and energy saver (it doesn't heat up your kitchen) and there is little mess.

- A food processor or blender is almost essential. It saves so much time and does a superior job of mixing and pureeing.
- Baking dishes should be metal or glass, never foil. Lower oven temperatures by 25° if you use glass pans.
- Because I have never been able to roll out a crust without a pastry cloth and rolling pin cover, I heartily recommend them.
- A timer that "roars and stomps" is essential!—so you can hear it from anywhere in the house.
- If convenience and time are important considerations, a freezer can be a good investment.
- An electric knife is not a necessity, but is certainly helpful with non-wheat breads. You can often find one at garage sales.

CONSIDERING INGREDIENTS . . .

Baking Powder

To test baking powder's effectiveness, add one teaspoon to 1/4 cup warm water. If bubbles form on the surface, the product is still good. You can expect it to last about a year. If you want to avoid using products with aluminum salts, you can shop at a health food store.

You can also make your own :

MIX 1 part cornstarch, 1 part cream of tartar, and 1/2 part baking soda *OR* 1 part arrowroot, 1 part cream of tartar, and 1/2 part baking soda.

Mix very well and store in an airtight container.

If recipe calls for 1 teaspoon regular baking powder, substitute 1 1/2 to 1 3/4 teaspoons homemade baking powder.

Use about 2 1/2 teaspoons baking powder to 1 cup wheat-free flour. Usually, use with sweet milk, not buttermilk.

When using homemade baking powder, do not allow your batter to stand before it is baked, because gas is given off the moment liquid is introduced. Make sure your oven is preheated. Get your batter mixed, into the pans, and into the oven posthaste. Don't even answer the telephone until the mixture is in the oven!

Baking Soda

Generally, use baking soda with something acidic like buttermilk or applesauce. To test its effectiveness, in a dish add a spoonful of soda to a spoonful of vinegar. If it bubbles, it's still active. Never use baking soda that has been used as a deodorizer in your refrigerator because its effectiveness will be reduced by moisture and odor.

Egg Substitutes

- Soak 1/2 pound apricots in 2 cups water overnight. Next morning beat or blend to the consistency of egg yolks (add water if needed), strain, and store in refrigerator. Substitute a generous tablespoon for each beaten egg called for in the recipe and blend into your dough.
- To 3 cups cold water add 1 cup ground flaxseed. Bring to a boil, stirring constantly. Boil 3 minutes. Cool. Keep in refrigerator in a closed jar. Substitute 1 tablespoon for each beaten egg. You can make all kinds of pancakes, muffins, and cookies using this substitute. It is more versatile than the other substitutes I give here.
- 1 1/2 tablespoons water   1 1/2 tablespoons oil
  1 teaspoon baking powder

Use this mixture for each egg called for, and add as you would add an egg. *(This recipe is courtesy of Kathy Forsyth, Mt. Lebanon, Penn.)*

Flours

Most recipes are grain free, with heavy emphasis on rice and chickpea (garbanzo bean) flour combinations. You will find that wheat-free baked products usually require longer and slower baking. Don't open the oven door during baking, and remember to allow baked goods to cool gradually before handling. Using an electric knife helps keep bread or cake from flattening as you slice.

Most flours mentioned can be readily purchased in health food stores; some can be found in stores that carry bulk foods, notably ethnic food stores. Freshly ground whole grain flour is best, or at least make every effort to buy flour freshly ground. I've been told to keep flour in the freezer, but I have good luck refrigerating it in cellophane or plastic bags with the air squeezed out.

Flour Substitutes

1 cup wheat flour equals:

7/8 cup amaranth flour	3/4 cup millet flour
3/4 cup white bean flour	3/4 cup oat flour
7/8 cup buckwheat flour	5/8 cup potato flour
7/8 cup chickpea (garbanzo) flour	3/4 cup potato starch
	7/8 cup rice flour
3/4 cup corn flour	3/4 cup soy flour
1 cup corn meal	3/4 cup tapioca flour

If you want to experiment with alternative flours, consult *The Allergy Self-Help Cookbook* by Marjorie Hurt Jones, RN (Rodale Press, 1984). The tables on cooking and baking with alternative flours are excellent.

Gluten

When wheat flour is mixed with liquid and warmed, the gluten expands to form elastic strands capable of trapping gas bubbles released by the yeast. This entrapment is what makes bread rise. Without gluten, bread is heavier and does not stick together. If you must avoid gluten, you must avoid not only wheat, but also oats, rye, barley, spelt, kamut, buckwheat, quinoa, and millet. They all contain some gluten.

When avoiding gluten, you will need other ingredients to make your baked goods stick together.

Xanthan gum is found in health food stores and is used extensively for holding baked goods together. *Eggs* will accomplish the same thing (but not the egg substitutes on p. 5), but too many eggs present other dangers, and people are seldom sensitive to xanthan gum. It is somewhat pricey, but a little seems to go a long way. I usually use 1 teaspoon xanthan gum for each cup of flour.

If xanthan gum is not available, substitute *pectin*. Pectin keeps breads, cakes, cookies, etc. from being crumbly. *Powdered pectin* (the kind you use to make jam with sugar) is best. Substitute 1 teaspoon for each teaspoon xanthan gum. The texture and taste will be slightly different, but still very good. If all you have on hand is *liquid pectin,* you can use that, also. Start by trying 1 teaspoon pectin for each teaspoon xanthan gum.

If you need to make your own pectin, see my recipe on p. 332. To use this recipe as a replacement for xanthan gum, boil the

liquid down to perhaps 1/4 of its volume and include it in the total liquid you add to your recipe. For example: If your recipe calls for 1 cup water, pour the pectin into the measuring cup and fill with enough water to make 1 cup. Because everyone will boil the pectin to a slightly different level, experiment with how much works to hold your baked product together.

Milk Substitutes

Health food stores and many large grocery stores carry soy, potato, and rice milks. Your health food store may also carry nut milks, or you can make them by processing 1/2 cup nuts (almonds and cashews are good choices) or seeds (sunflower) in 2 cups water, blending until creamy.

These milks will taste good on cereal and in any of the recipes, but water works, also. However, when you substitute juice or water in a bread-type recipe you sacrifice lightness, but the baked good can be just as tasty.

Salt

Salt keeps yeast from running amuck. Too much salt, however, will kill the yeast in your bread recipes.

Shortening

If you have to avoid gluten, you need to avoid hydrogenated shortening as well. Your choices for bread making, then, are oil, butter, or lard. Lard gives a quality and texture not found with other shortening. You usually use less and the taste is worth it, but because it is animal fat, you should not use it extensively.

You may prefer to use butter because it adds immeasurably to the taste, but margarine or solid shortening can be substituted for butter in all the recipes. Read the labels to be sure you are using a product you can tolerate. Dr. Green warns against using margarine and shortening because they contain trans fatty acids, which are not good for you.

Sugar

I have chosen recipes that require less sugar, but some sweetener is necessary in bread recipes to make yeast raise. Like salt, however, too much sugar will kill the yeast. Sugar gives structure and lightness to a bread-type recipe, so a recipe using honey may taste very good, but the product will be heavier than if you used sugar.

Sugar Substitutes

You can substitute honey or molasses, rice syrup or maple syrup. Honey may be substituted for sugar in most recipes without any liquid adjustments, but when substituting sugar for honey, use 1/2 the amount called for and lower the cooking temperature by 25°.

Powdered Sugar

Powdered sugar has cornstarch in it. Just in case you cannot tolerate corn, here is a substitute to help you with your candy recipes. You may need to experiment a bit with quantity to get the right amount of sugar.

Superfine Sugar

You can make superfine sugar by processing granulated sugar in a blender for 1 minute. Store in airtight container.

Tamari

Tamari is a wheat-free soy sauce (Yes, there is wheat in other soy sauces!) you can find in health food stores and some Asian markets.

Thickeners

Arrowroot Flour

Arrowroot flour (also called arrowroot starch or just arrowroot) is a thickener that can be used for soups, sauces, and puddings. It has no flavor of its own and is the easiest starch to digest. It can be found at your health food store.

Arrowroot is best used at the end of cooking just before boiling because continued heating will cause it to lose its thickening ability. Dissolve arrowroot in 1/4 cup liqud from your recipe and add as recipe directs.

Arrowroot is also good to use as a coating before frying because it makes a lighter and crispier coating.

Cornstarch

The advantage of cornstarch is that it thickens after reaching its boiling point. It is very effective, but only if you are not allergic to corn! Dissolve cornstarch in 1/4 cup liquid from your recipe and add as recipe directs. For 1 tablespoon cornstarch, you may substitute 1 tablespoon arrowroot flour, 2 tablespoons other flour, or 2 tablespoons tapioca.

Flour

With flour, you bring the mixture to a boil. It will thicken about 2 to 3 minutes after boiling. The flavor of your dish will change, depending on what kind of flour you use.

Tapioca

Combine tapioca with fruit and liquids and allow to stand 5 minutes. Bring to a boil and boil 1 minute, stirring constantly. Remove from heat and cool. Tapioca thickens as it cools.

Vinegar

Clear vinegar is made from grains and should be avoided. You can substitute cider or wine vinegars.

Water

Unless otherwise specified, warm water should be 110° to 115°.

Yeast

One packet of dry yeast equals one yeast cake equals 1 tablespoon dry yeast. Keep yeast in your refrigerator and bring to room temperature before using. One tablespoon yeast will raise as much as 8 cups of flour. Dry yeast is much more stable than yeast cakes, lasting as long as a year in refrigeration.

To test the liveliness of your yeast, add a pinch to a little warm water and 1/2 teaspoon sugar or honey. If it bubbles and foams, it is working.

ABOUT ALLERGIES . . .

Altough no one can help you as well as a doctor whose area of expertise is food allergies, if you do have allergies or sensitivities, be aware of the need for food rotation. Eating the same foods day after day can bring about sensitivities to those foods. Thus, if you use oat or corn flour in all your baked goods, you can become sensitive to those grains. To be on the safe side, try to rotate your food choices so you do not eat a grain or sensitive food more often than once every two to four days.

Now your freezer really helps. For example, when you make Amish Friendship Bread for dinner, divide what is left into lunch-size servings, freeze in plastic bags or wrap, and label.

Some people have special shelves in their freezers for food rotation. Label a shelf or container oat, corn, rice, or bean flour. On day 1, eat from shelf 1. On day 2, eat from shelf 2 and so on. Dr. Green says that rotation should keep foods of the same group at least two days apart, so you may want to skip a day between rice and garbanzo products and have no grain or legumes in between. Some people can get away with eating grain daily. But, he cautions, "I see much rice sensitivity from over-dosing on rice."

With everything packaged and labeled, you can grab some bread and take it with you to your breakfast meeting. You can always have something delicious whenever everyone else is going for doughnuts.

MEASURING TIPS . . .

I never knew there was a difference between a liquid measuring cup and a dry measuring cup. To tell the truth, I do not think it makes much difference which you use—most of the time. However, when you are measuring dry ingredients, for bread in particular, follow these instructions:

- For liquid ingredients use a multicup measure.

- For dry ingredients use an exact 1/4, 1/3, 1/2, or 1 cup measure. Tap the side of the cup a couple of times with a straight-edge knife, and level off the ingredients by running the flat side of the knife over the top of the cup.

- Never use the measuring cup as a flour scoop. It will pack in too much flour, affecting your accuracy.

Breads

"A LOAF OF BREAD," THE WALRUS SAID,
"IS WHAT WE CHIEFLY NEED."

—Lewis Carroll,
Alice Through the Looking Glass

This mix makes so many good things and saves so much time.

BISCUIT MIX

3 1/2 cups rice flour	1 tablespoon salt
3 1/2 cups bean flour (see note)	2 teaspoons cream of tartar
5 tablespoons baking powder	1 teaspoon baking soda
4 teaspoons xanthan gum	2 1/4 cups shortening

MIX well all ingredients except shortening.

ADD shortening and MIX well.

STORE in sealed container in refrigerator or if on a shelf no longer than a month.

Note: For the bean flour, you may substitute
   *1 3/4 cups potato starch
   and 1 3/4 cups tapioca flour
   OR
   3 1/2 cups millet flour*

This mix makes wonderful Impossible Pies, pancakes, waffles, dumplings, and coffee cakes.

BISCUITS

3 cups Biscuit Mix (p. 14)
2/3 to 1 cup water or milk

PREHEAT oven to 350°.

COMBINE ingredients and LET STAND 5 minutes.

KNEAD dough about 15 times, adding rice flour if sticky.

ROLL out to 3/4 inch thickness. CUT with floured biscuit cutter.

PLACE about 1 inch apart on unbuttered cookie sheet.

BAKE at 350° for 25 minutes.

You can save time by spooning unkneaded dough into an 8-inch round cake pan and baking about 45 minutes.

CHEESE BISCUITS

2 cups Biscuit Mix (p. 14)
2 tablespoons onion flakes
2/3 cup water or milk

1/2 cup grated cheddar or
Parmesan cheese
Poppy seeds

PREHEAT oven to 325°.

GREASE a 9 x 11-inch or 9-inch round pan.

COMBINE biscuit mix, onion flakes, and water or milk.

SPREAD in greased pan.

SPRINKLE cheese on top. TOP with lots of poppy seeds.

BAKE at 325° for 40 minutes.

This recipe can make dough or batter.

SHORTCAKE

3 cups Biscuit Mix (p. 14)
2 tablespoons granulated sugar
1/4 cup butter or
   margarine, melted
1/2 cup water or milk

1 egg, beaten
1/2 cup additional water
Fruit
Whipped cream

PREHEAT oven to 375°.

COMBINE biscuit mix and sugar in medium bowl.

COMBINE melted butter, water or milk, and egg.

ADD to dry ingredients with fork until just moistened, to make dough.

ADD additional water and MIX well to make batter.

For dough:

KNEAD 8 - 10 times on lightly floured surface.

ROLL dough to 3/4-inch thickness.

CUT about 6 circles with lightly floured cutter.

PLACE on unbuttered cookie sheet.

BAKE at 375° about 20 minutes until browned.

TOP with fruit and whipped cream.

For batter:

GREASE 8-inch square baking pan.

POUR batter into pan.

BAKE about 20 minutes until browned.

CUT into 6 pieces.

TOP with fruit and whipped cream.

CINNAMON ROLLS

3 cups Biscuit Mix (p. 14)
2/3 to 1 cup water or milk
Butter, melted
Cinnamon

Brown sugar
Powdered sugar
Water or orange juice

PREHEAT oven to 350°.

GREASE cookie sheet.

COMBINE biscuit mix and water or milk and LET STAND 5 minutes.

KNEAD dough about 15 times, adding rice flour if sticky.

ROLL into a 1/2-inch thick rectangle.

SPREAD with melted butter.

ADD cinnamon and brown sugar to taste and ROLL UP lengthwise.

SLICE roll into 3/4-inch slices and LAY them flat on greased cookie sheet.

BAKE at 350° for 15 minutes.

COOL, then SPREAD with mixture of powdered sugar and a few drops water or orange juice.

If you haven't any Biscuit Mix, here's a recipe for one batch of . . .

BAKING POWDER BISCUITS

3/4 cup rice flour
3/4 cup bean flour
1 1/2 teaspoons xanthan gum
4 teaspoons baking powder

1 teaspoon salt
1/4 cup shortening
3/4 cup water or milk

PREHEAT oven to 425°.

KNEAD for 20 seconds, adding rice flour if dough is sticky.

ROLL 3/4 inch thick.

CUT out biscuits with floured cutter.

PLACE on greased cookie sheet.

ALLOW biscuits to stand 10 minutes in a warm place before baking (if you have time!)

BAKE at 425° for 25 minutes.

OR

SPOON batter into 8-inch round pan.

BAKE at 350° for 40 minutes.

The lemon rind really makes these special.

LEMON SCONES

1 1/2 cups rice flour*	1/4 cup honey
1 cup bean flour*	2 eggs
5 teaspoons baking powder*	1 tablespoon grated lemon rind
2 teaspoons xanthan gum*	1/3 cup + additional lemon juice
1/2 cup butter	1/2 cup water

*OR use 2 1/2 cups commercial wheat-free biscuit mix or
Biscuit Mix 2 (p. 23).

PREHEAT oven to 400°.

COMBINE flours, baking powder, and xanthan gum with butter
until mixture is crumbly.

MIX in a small bowl honey, eggs, lemon rind, lemon juice, and water.

ADD liquid mixture to dry ingredients and STIR with a fork.

TURN dough onto lightly floured surface and KNEAD 10 times.

PAT dough into round shape 1 inch thick and BRUSH with additional lemon juice.

SPRINKLE with 1 tablespoon sugar.

CUT into wedges and PLACE on ungreased cookie sheet.

BAKE at 400° for 30 minutes.

OR

PLACE dough in 8-inch round ungreased pan.

BAKE at 375° for 50 minutes.

BEER MUFFINS

> *2 cups Biscuit Mix (p. 14)*
> *2 tablespoons granulated sugar*
> *6 ounces beer at room temperature*

PREHEAT oven to 350°.

GREASE muffins pans.

MIX all ingredients together and KNEAD on a board about 6 times.

DROP by tablespoonfuls into greased muffin pans.

BAKE at 350° for 35 to 40 minutes.

PANCAKES

> *2 1/4 cups Biscuit Mix (p. 14)*
> *1 tablespoon granulated sugar (see note)*
> *1 egg, beaten*
> *1 1/2 cups milk or water*

MIX biscuit mix and sugar.

ADD egg and milk or water, and MIX well.

LET rest 5 to 10 minutes.

SPREAD 1/4 cup batter on oiled hot griddle.

COOK 3 to 4 minutes until browned on both sides.

Note: Sugar helps pancakes to brown.

Yield: 10 to 12 pancakes

WAFFLES

The pancake recipe can be used for waffles. Pour batter onto preheated waffle iron and bake until brown. Makes about 3 waffles.

Dr. Green's recipe for buckwheat pancakes makes very good bread for sandwiches. Make a big batch and freeze it. Buckwheat contains gluten.

BUCKWHEAT PANCAKES

1 cup buckwheat flour	*1 teaspoon baking soda*
1 cup rice flour	*1 egg*
2 cups soy milk or water	*2 to 3 teaspoons brown sugar*
1/4 cup sesame seeds (optional)	

MIX all ingredients thoroughly.

SPREAD 1/4 cup batter for each pancake on oiled hot griddle.

COOK 2 to 3 minutes each side.

Yield: about 16 pancakes

For frying fish or . . .

FRYING BATTER

1 cup corn or bean flour	*1 cup milk or water*
Salt and pepper	*1 beaten egg*

COMBINE ingredients.

Note: COAT both sides of fish with batter. FRY in hot oil until brown.

ORANGE COFFEE CAKE

2 cups Biscuit Mix (p. 14)
3 tablespoons
  granulated sugar
1/4 teaspoon nutmeg
1 tablespoon grated
  orange peel
1 egg, slightly beaten
2/3 cup milk or water
3 tablespoons orange
  marmalade
3 tablespoons orange juice
  concentrate, frozen or thawed

Topping:
  1/4 cup cold butter
  1/3 cup Biscuit Mix
  1/4 cup brown sugar

Powdered Sugar Icing:
  1 cup powdered sugar
  1 tablespoon hot water
  1/4 teaspoon vanilla

PREHEAT oven to 400°.

GREASE and FLOUR 9-inch round pan.

COMBINE biscuit mix with sugar, nutmeg, and orange peel.

BEAT egg with milk in another bowl.

ADD liquid mixture to dry mixture to dampen.

SPREAD batter in pan.

BLEND marmalade and orange juice concentrate in a small bowl.

SPREAD evenly on top of batter.

MIX topping ingredients in another bowl until crumbly.

SPRINKLE evenly over batter.

REDUCE heat to 375° and BAKE for 40 minutes.

COMBINE icing ingredients. (THIN with drops of water if necessary.)

DRIZZLE icing on cake.

SERVE warm.

If you prefer not to use hydrogenated shortenings such as Crisco or margarine, this recipe provides the convenience of a mix but lets you add the shortening, such as oil, later. Mixing instructions will be different.

BISCUIT MIX 2

· (Without Shortening)

> *3 1/2 cups rice flour*
> *3 1/2 cups bean flour (see note)*
> *5 tablespoons baking powder*
> *4 teaspoons xanthan gum*
> *1 tablespoon salt*
> *2 teaspoons cream of tartar*
> *1 teaspoon baking soda*

MIX all ingredients well.

STORE in sealed container in refrigerator or on a shelf for several months.

Note: If you cannot tolerate bean flour or if you need to rotate flours, substitute the following for the bean flour:

> *1 3/4 cups potato starch and*
> *1 3/4 cups tapioca flour*
> OR
> *3 1/2 cups millet flour*

If you must avoid gluten, avoid millet.

This mix makes wonderful Impossible Pies, pancakes, waffles, dumplings, and coffee cakes.

*Recipes for Biscuit Mix 2 allow you to add shortening to the mix.
The following recipes are for Biscuit Mix 2.*

BISCUITS 2

2 1/2 cups Biscuit Mix 2 (p. 23)
1/2 cup shortening or 1/3 cup oil
2/3 to 1 cup water or milk

PREHEAT oven to 350°.

MIX all ingredients.

KNEAD 10 times on lightly floured board.

ROLL to 3/4-inch thickness.

CUT with floured cutter.

BAKE at 350° for 25 minutes or until browned.

PANCAKES 2

1 egg
2 tablespoons granulated sugar
1/4 cup oil
1 1/2 cups Biscuit Mix 2 (p. 23)
4 cups water

MIX egg, sugar, and oil.

ADD biscuit mix and enough water to make batter as thin or thick
as you like (More water makes thinner pancakes.).

SPREAD 1/4 cup batter for each pancake on oiled hot griddle.

COOK 2 to 3 minutes each side until browned on both sides.

Yield: about 18 pancakes

SHORTCAKE 2

2 1/2 cups Biscuit Mix 2 (p. 23)
2 tablespoons granulated sugar
1/2 cup melted butter
   or 1/4 cup oil
1/2 cup water or milk
1 egg, beaten
Fruit
Whipped topping

PREHEAT oven to 375°.

GREASE cookie sheet.

COMBINE biscuit mix and sugar in bowl.

COMBINE in another bowl butter or oil, water or milk, and egg.

ADD to dry ingredients until just moistened.

KNEAD 10 times on lightly floured board.

ROLL to 3/4-inch thickness and CUT with floured cutter.

BAKE on greased cookie sheet about 20 minutes until brown.

TOP with your favorite fruit and whipped topping.

A British version of an American favorite—biscuits—these scones are even better the next day.

OAT SCONES

1/3 cup oil
2 tablespoons honey
2 tablespoons warm water
1 tablespoon lemon juice
1 to 2 cups oat flour, divided
1/4 cup rice flour

2 tablespoons baking powder
1/2 teaspoon baking soda
2 teaspoons xanthan gum
1/3 cup currants or raisins
1/3 cup, divided + extra
  uncooked quick rolled oats

PREHEAT oven to 325°.

WARM oil, honey, water, and lemon juice in 3-quart saucepan until honey melts.

COMBINE 3/4 cup oat flour with rice flour, baking powder, baking soda, and xanthan gum.

STIR into oil mixture.

ADD currants or raisins and BEAT 50 strokes.

Gradually ADD enough oat flour to form a ball that isn't sticky.

DIVIDE dough into 2 balls.

SCATTER 1/2 rolled oats on a board.

ROLL 1 ball until covered with oats.

FLATTEN into 6-inch circle about 3/4 inch thick.

TURN to evenly COAT with oats.

SCATTER extra oats on ungreased cookie sheet.

PLACE dough on cookie sheet.

CUT into 8 wedges, but do not separate wedges.

REPEAT with remaining dough ball.

BAKE at 325° for 25 minutes or until golden brown.

COOL on cookie sheet for 30 minutes.

The recipe for the perfect loaf of wheat-free bread is elusive, but the experimenting goes on. This bread rises beautifully and is good with creamed chicken or fish.

CORN BREAD

1 cup yellow corn meal	2 tablespoons baking powder
1 cup rice flour	1/3 cup oil
1/4 cup granulated sugar	1 egg
1 teaspoon salt	2 cups milk or water
2 teaspoons xanthan gum	Grated cheese (optional)

PREHEAT oven to 350°.

BUTTER generously 8-inch square pan.

COMBINE dry ingredients in large bowl.

COMBINE liquid ingredients in another bowl.

STIR liquid ingredients into dry ingredients until just blended.

POUR into buttered pan.

Optional: TOP with grated cheese before baking.

BAKE at 350° for 40 minutes or until done. SERVE warm.

You can chill the batter overnight.

DUTCH BABIES

3 large eggs
6 tablespoons rice flour
1 tablespoon granulated sugar
6 tablespoons milk or water

3 tablespoons butter
Powdered sugar
1 lemon

MIX eggs, flour, granulated sugar, and milk or water in processor until smooth.

PUT butter into 10 or 12-inch frying pan.

SET pan in cold oven and HEAT to 425°.

ADD batter when butter is melted.

BAKE until pancake puffs at edges, about 15 minutes.

CUT into wedges and DUST with powdered sugar.

SQUEEZE on lemon juice.

You can make part of this pastry the day before baking.

PLUM BREAKFAST PASTRY

3/4 cup rice flour
3/4 cup bean flour
2 teaspoons xanthan gum
1/2 teaspoon salt
1/2 cup mashed potatoes
1 cup butter

1 cup non-dairy sour cream
8 to 10 ounces plum jam
2/3 cup chopped walnuts
1 cup coconut
Powdered sugar

PREHEAT oven to 325°.

GREASE cookie sheet.

COMBINE flours, potatoes, xanthan gum, and salt.

CUT in butter as for a pie crust.

MIX in sour cream.

REFRIGERATE overnight, if desired.

LET STAND at room temperature 1 hour, if refrigerated.

CUT dough in half and ROLL each half into 10 x 15-inch rectangle.

SPREAD each with 1/2 jam, nuts, and coconut.

ROLL up lengthwise, jellyroll style.

BAKE on greased cookie sheet at 325° for 55 minutes. COOL.

SPRINKLE with powdered sugar and SLICE.

This coffee cake is sugar free.

CINNAMON RAISIN COFFEE CAKE

1/3 ripe banana, mashed
1/2 cup butter or margarine
3 large eggs
1 teaspoon vanilla extract
1 1/2 cups water
1 1/2 cups rice flour
1 teaspoon baking soda
4 teaspoons baking powder
3 teaspoons xanthan gum
1 1/2 cups raisins

Topping:
1/3 cup raisins or
  chopped dates
1/3 cup chopped walnuts
  or sliced almonds
1/3 cup flaked coconut
1 teaspoon cinnamon

PREHEAT oven to 300°.

OIL and FLOUR 9 x 13-inch pan.

MASH bananas with butter.

ADD eggs, vanilla, and water.

BEAT mixture.

MEASURE in flours, baking soda, baking powder, xanthan gum, and raisins. POUR into oiled and floured pan.

COMBINE topping ingredients and SPRINKLE over batter.

BAKE at 300° for 25 minutes.

Summer's coming when you can pick strawberries at the farm just down the road. Pick enough for this lovely bread.

STRAWBERRY BREAD

12 ounces (1 pint) fresh strawberries
or about 1 1/2 cups thawed
2/3 cup rice flour
2/3 cup bean flour
1/2 teaspoon baking soda
1 teaspoon xanthan gum
1 teaspoon cinnamon

Pinch salt
1 cup granulated sugar
2 eggs
1/2 cup vegetable oil
1 teaspoon vanilla
1/2 cup chopped nuts
(walnuts are good)

PREHEAT oven to 325°.

GREASE medium loaf pan.

SLICE and slightly MASH strawberries, SET ASIDE.

COMBINE flours, baking soda, xanthan gum, cinnamon, and salt and SET ASIDE.

BEAT sugar, eggs, and oil in large bowl.

ADD flour mixture to sugar mixture and MIX quickly.

FOLD in strawberries, vanilla, and nuts.

POUR into greased loaf pan and PUT into oven immediately.

BAKE at 325° about 10 minutes.

CONTINUE baking at 300° about 1 hour 35 minutes.

COOL in pan.

*Eggs add richness to this bread, but you can omit them and add 1/3
cup water. Wonderful with coffee, a dessert wine, or cheese.
Slices also make good toast.*

ITALIAN BISCUIT BREAD

1 cup butter or margarine
1 cup granulated sugar
3 eggs
3 tablespoons sweet Marsala
  wine (see note)
1 1/2 teaspoons vanilla extract
Pinch salt
3/4 cup bean flour
3/4 cup rice flour

1 teaspoon xanthan gum
1/3 cup chopped dried
  apricots
1/3 cup chopped dates
1/3 cup chopped prunes or
  dried figs
1/2 cup chopped roasted
  hazelnuts

PREHEAT oven to 325°.

GREASE 4 x 9-inch loaf pan.

COMBINE butter and sugar in large bowl.

ADD eggs, one at a time, BEATING well after each addition.

ADD wine, vanilla, and salt and SET ASIDE.

COMBINE flours and xanthan gum.

MIX dried fruits and nuts with flour mixture.

ADD to batter.

POUR into greased loaf pan.

BAKE at 325° until golden, about 70 minutes.

COOL in pan for 10 minutes.

REMOVE from pan onto wire rack.

Note: Substitute any sweet dessert wine, if desired.

This bread is wonderfully moist.

PUMPKIN BREAD

1 1/2 cups bean flour
1 1/2 cups rice flour
1 1/2 teaspoons salt
1 teaspoon cinnamon
1 teaspoon nutmeg
2 teaspoons baking soda
3 teaspoons xanthan gum
2 cups pureed cooked or
   canned pumpkin

1 cup honey or
  2 1/3 cups granulated sugar
  + 2/3 cup water
1 cup corn oil
1/2 cup water
4 eggs

PREHEAT oven to 325°.

GREASE and FLOUR two medium loaf pans.

STIR together in large bowl flours, salt, cinnamon, nutmeg, baking soda, and xanthan gum.

STIR together pumpkin, honey or sugar and water, corn oil, and water.

ADD eggs one at a time, BEATING well after each addition.

MAKE a well in center of flour mixture.

ADD pumpkin mixture and STIR.

POUR into greased and floured loaf pans.

BAKE at 325° for 1 hour.

COOL for 10 minutes.

Dr. Green claimed not to like being a guinea pig, but every last crumb of this bread disappeared!

ZUCCHINI BREAD

3/4 cup rice flour
3/4 cup bean flour
2 teaspoons xanthan gum
1/2 teaspoon baking powder
1/2 teaspoon baking soda
1/2 teaspoon salt
1 teaspoon cinnamon

2 eggs
1 cup honey or 1 1/3 cups
granulated sugar (see note)
2/3 cup cooking oil
2 teaspoons vanilla
1 1/3 cups shredded zucchini
1/2 cup chopped pecans

PREHEAT oven to 325°.

GREASE 9 x 5 x 3-inch loaf pan.

SIFT together flours, xanthan gum, baking powder, baking soda, salt, and cinnamon. SET ASIDE.

BEAT eggs until blended.

ADD sugar or honey and oil gradually, MIXING well after each addition.

BLEND in vanilla.

STIR in zucchini and nuts.

ADD dry ingredients.

MIX until dry ingredients are just moistened.

POUR into greased loaf pan.

BAKE at 325° for 1 hour or until cake tester comes out clean.

REMOVE from pan onto wire rack and COOL 10 minutes.

Note: Reducing granulated sugar to 1/2 cup brown sugar tastes less sweet, but cake will not rise as well.

The kids love Sylvia's sweet bread.

AUNT SYLVIA'S MONDAL BREAD

1 egg
1/2 cup + additional
  granulated sugar
1/4 cup oil
1/2 teaspoon vanilla
3/4 cup oat flour or combined
  rice and bean flours

1/2 teaspoon baking powder
1/4 teaspoon baking soda
1 teaspoon xanthan gum
1/2 cup EACH
  chocolate chips, raisins, nuts
Cinnamon

PREHEAT oven to 350°.

GREASE 8-inch round pan.

MIX egg, sugar, oil, and vanilla and BEAT well.

MIX in another bowl flour, baking powder, xanthan gum, and
baking soda.

ADD liquid mix to dry mix.

ADD chocolate chips, raisins, and nuts and MIX.

BAKE in greased pan at 350° for 35 to 40 minutes.

SPRINKLE top with sugar and cinnamon.

BAKE at 350° another 10 minutes.

CUT when cool.

This is the kind of food you keep in the freezer ready for a business meeting or social get-together. It's as good as what anyone else will have (maybe better)!

BRAN LOAF

(You will need additional time.)
1 cup rice or corn bran
1 cup raisins
3/4 cup granulated sugar
1 1/2 cups water
3/4 cup rice flour
3/4 cup bean flour
1 1/2 teaspoons xanthan gum
3 teaspoons baking powder

PREHEAT oven to 325° for muffins or 350° for loaf.

GREASE muffin pans or medium loaf pan.

MIX bran, raisins, sugar, and water in bowl.

LET stand 2 hours or overnight.

ADD flours, xanthan gum, and baking powder.

POUR into greased loaf pan and BAKE at 350° for 1 hour.

OR

FILL muffin pans nearly full and BAKE at 325° for 35 minutes.

Yield: 12 muffins or one loaf

This bread can be baked or steamed. Steamed bread is moister.

BROWN BREAD

1 1/2 cups bean flour	2 teaspoons baking soda
1 1/2 cups rye flour	1/2 teaspoon salt
1 cup corn meal	2 cups buttermilk or applesauce
1/2 cup granulated sugar	1 cup mild molasses
1 teaspoon xanthan gum	1 cup raisins

PREHEAT oven to 375°.

GREASE about five 16-ounce fruit cans.

COMBINE flours, corn meal, sugar, and xanthan gum.

MIX baking soda and salt into buttermilk or applesauce.

ADD to flour mixture, then ADD molasses and raisins.

POUR about 1 cup batter into each can.

To Bake:

BAKE 30 minutes or until cake tester comes out clean.

REMOVE from oven. COOL 5 minutes.

REMOVE bread from cans onto wire rack and COOL.

WRAP securely and STORE overnight in refrigerator before serving.

To Steam:

COVER each can tightly with aluminum foil and TIE with string.
Rubber bands also work.

PLACE on rack or jar rings set in large Dutch oven.

POUR in boiling water to depth of 1 inch.

COVER pot and SIMMER over low heat, STEAMING bread until
done, 2 1/2 to 3 hours.

ADD more boiling water as needed.

REMOVE bread from cans onto wire rack and COOL.

Amaranth flour has a distinctive flavor that goes well with fruit.

GRAIN-FREE BROWN BREAD

*1 cup + 2 tablespoons
  amaranth flour
1/4 cup arrowroot flour
1 teaspoon baking soda
1/2 teaspoon powdered ginger
1 teaspoon xanthan gum*

*1/2 cup currants or
  chopped prunes
1/2 cup walnuts, almonds,
  or Brazil nuts
3/4 cup boiling water
1/4 cup honey or molasses
1 tablespoon lemon juice*

GREASE 1-quart mold or 1-quart coffee can.

FILL deep kettle or canner with 5 inches water. BRING to a boil.

COMBINE flours, baking soda, ginger, and xanthan gum in large bowl. STIR in currants or prunes.

GRIND nuts to a powder in blender or processor.

ADD water and BLEND.

ADD more water to nuts if necessary to make 1 cup liquid.

ADD honey or molasses and lemon juice to liquid.

COMBINE liquid with flour mixture, STIRRING quickly to blend. Do not overmix. POUR into greased mold or can.

COVER with aluminum foil or wax paper and TIE securely with string.

SET on rack or jar rings in kettle. ADD additional boiling water to canner until it reaches halfway up sides of mold.

COVER and STEAM for 2 hours, keeping water boiling gently.

REMOVE mold from pot. COOL about 15 minutes.

REMOVE from mold onto wire rack.

In the 1800's the hard crust helped preserve the bread. If it is too tough for you, use it for dunking. The flavor is great.

OLD FASHIONED INDIAN RYE BREAD

3 cups corn meal
1 teaspoon salt
1/2 cup molasses
1 cup boiling water or
  boiling milk
1 teaspoon butter, softened

1 1/2 cups cold buttermilk
4 cups rye flour
2 teaspoons baking soda
1/2 cup mashed Irish potatoes
Raisins (optional)
Butter

PREHEAT oven to 375°.

GREASE 8-inch round pan.

MIX corn meal, salt, and molasses in large bowl.

POUR boiling water or milk over corn meal mixture.

ADD cold buttermilk to rye flour and baking soda in another bowl.

MIX buttermilk mixture into corn meal mixture.

ADD potatoes and raisins, if using.

KNEAD in bowl until firm, then PLACE in greased pan.

PLACE shallow pan of water in bottom of oven and COVER lightly with tinfoil, to help reduce browning.

BAKE (without rising) at 375° for 2 hours.

RUB with butter when done and COVER with a towel to retain moisture.

After tasting fry bread made by Warm Springs Indians,
I tried it with alternative flours.
The best is oat flour, with bean flour a close second.

INDIAN FRY BREAD

1 1/2 cups oat or bean flour	*2 tablespoons baking powder*
1 1/2 cups rice flour	*1 teaspoon salt*
1 tablespoon granulated sugar	*2 teaspoons shortening*
3 teaspoons xanthan gum	*1 1/2 cups cold water*
	Oil

MIX dry ingredients.

CUT in shortening.

ADD enough water to make thick dough.

KNEAD well.

HEAT oil in deep fryer or Dutch oven to 350°.

BREAK off handfuls of dough and FRY until golden brown.

DRAIN.

SERVE warm.

Note: Excellent with blackberry jam.

CROUTONS

LINE a microwavable platter with wax paper.
SPREAD 2 slices wheat-free bread on both sides with a thin layer of
Dijon-type mustard.
CUT into small cubes and PLACE on wax paper.
MICROWAVE on high 1 1/2 minutes.
STIR well and MICROWAVE another 1 1/2 minutes or until bread
feels dry.

DUMPLINGS

1 cup Biscuit Mix (p. 14)   *1/4 cup grated cheddar cheese*
1/2 cup milk or water   *(optional)*
                                                    2 teaspoons dried parsley
                                                    (optional)

MIX grated cheese and/or dried parsley, if using, into biscuit mix.
STIR milk or water into biscuit mix to form stiff dough.
DROP by spoonfuls into simmering stew or soup.
COVER and COOK 15 minutes.
Yield: 5 large dumplings

These crepes make a handy and flavorful substitute for sandwiches.
You can wrap them around almost any filling.

FAUX CREPES

1/2 cup bean flour (see note)
1/2 teaspoon salt
1/2 teaspoon xanthan
 gum or 1 egg
2/3 cup water
2 teaspoons olive oil, divided

Garlic Butter:
 6 tablespoons unsalted butter
 1 garlic clove, chopped
 Parsley, basil, or garlic
  powder (optional)

SIFT flour, salt, and xanthan gum, if using, into mixing bowl.

ADD half the water and egg, if using.

MIX with a whisk.

STIR in remaining water and LET REST 10 minutes.

PREHEAT oven to 200°.

HEAT nonstick 8 or 9-inch skillet over medium high heat.

BRUSH skillet lightly with 1 teaspoon oil.

When skillet is hot, POUR in all batter and ROTATE pan to spread batter evenly. Batter should sizzle.

COOK 2 minutes until batter is brown at edges.

POUR on remaining 1 teaspoon oil and COOK 5 more minutes.

TURN crepe. (Fingers work best!)

COOK 5 minutes.

REMOVE crepe, COVER with towel, and KEEP WARM in oven until ready to serve.

COMBINE garlic butter ingredients and WARM.

SERVE crepe immediately with garlic butter or fruit.

Note: You may substitute buckwheat, oat, or amaranth flour for the bean flour.

Several countries offer delicious recipes without using wheat.

NORWEGIAN LEFSE

(You will need additional time.)
   2 cups hot mashed potatoes
   2 tablespoons butter or margarine
   1 tablespoon water or rice milk
   1 teaspoon salt
   1 cup rice flour, divided

BEAT together potatoes, butter or margarine, water or rice milk, and salt.

COVER and CHILL 2 hours.

TURN onto lightly floured surface.

SPRINKLE with 1/2 cup flour.

KNEAD 8 to 10 minutes, gradually ADDING remaining 1/2 cup flour.

DIVIDE dough into portions about the size of golf balls.

ROLL to 6 to 8-inch circle.

WRAP dough around rolling pin and UNWRAP into hot greased skillet or griddle.

COOK 4 to 6 minutes until lightly browned, TURNING once.

BUTTER and SPRINKLE with sugar and cinnamon.

ROLL up to eat as bread or WRAP around food.

NOODLES

(You will need additional time.)
1 3/4 cups rice flour (see note)
1 3/4 cups bean flour (see note)
3 teaspoons xanthan gum
1 tablespoon salt
4 whole eggs
5 egg yolks
About 1/8 cup cold water
1 tablespoon butter or olive oil

MIX together all ingredients.

ADD enough water, 1 teaspoonful at a time, to MIX dough into ball.

COVER with tea towel and LET REST 45 minutes.

ROLL dough until very thin. LET REST 20 to 30 minutes.

ROLL up dough and SLICE into noodles with sharp knife or pasta or pizza cutter.

COOK in stock pot in boiling water 12 to 15 minutes. DRAIN.

ADD butter or oil. TOSS before serving.

Note: You may substitute 2 1/2 cups rice flour, 2/3 cup potato starch, and 1/3 cup tapioca flour for the rice and bean flours.

Note: A pasta machine is a luxury, but it provides uniform thickness and size to noodles, spaghetti, and macaroni.

Instead of pasta made with wheat, try rice noodles from your Asian grocer. They are very convenient.

RICE NOODLES

SOAK rice noodles in warm water 15 minutes or until tender but still firm.

DRAIN and COOK in boiling water 1 minute.

DRAIN and RINSE thoroughly with cold water.

RICE NOODLE SALAD

ADD tiny shrimp, diced cucumber, sliced scallions, and chopped roasted nuts to cooked rice noodles.

ADD oil and wine or rice vinegar salad dressing and TOSS.

SPRINKLE with mint.

BUCKWHEAT SPAGHETTI

1 cup buckwheat flour	*4 tablespoons water*
4 teaspoons + 1 tablespoon oil	*Salted water*

COMBINE flour, 4 teaspoons oil, and water to form a firm dough.

KNEAD 10 minutes.

PLACE dough on oiled surface and ROLL as thinly as possible.

CUT into fine strips.

BOIL salted water in large saucepan and ADD 1 tablespoon oil.

COOK strips until tender, about 3 minutes.

DRAIN and SERVE with sauce.

CRACKERS

(You will need additional time.)
  2 cups amaranth, bean, oat, or corn flour (see note)
  1 teaspoon baking powder or baking soda
  1 teaspoon salt
  1/2 teaspoon favorite seasoning (optional)
  1/3 cup olive, safflower, corn, or vegetable oil
  About 2/3 cup cold water

MIX flour, baking powder or baking soda, salt and seasoning, if using.

ADD oil and MIX with fork until crumbly.

ADD water slowly, as needed, and FORM into 2 balls.

CHILL 2 to 3 hours.

PREHEAT oven to 350°.

GREASE cookie sheet lightly.

ROLL out 1 ball to about 1/4 inch on cookie sheet. (SPRINKLE dough with flour if it sticks to rolling pin.)

CUT into 2-inch squares.

PRICK several times with fork.

BAKE at 350° for 10 minutes or until brown. (Watch carefully to avoid burning.)

SAVE any crumbs in tightly-covered container in freezer for breading, stuffing, etc.

Note: 3 tablespoons amaranth flour has a calcium content equal to 1/2 cup milk.

You may want to triple this recipe!

SUNFLOWER CRACKERS

1 cup ground sunflower seeds
1/2 cup shredded coconut
1/4 cup cold water
1 teaspoon xanthan gum or pectin
Seasoning or salt (optional)

GREASE cookie sheet.

COMBINE seeds, coconut, water, and xanthan gum or pectin.

PAT dough onto greased cookie sheet.

PLACE wax paper on top of dough.

ROLL dough to edges of cookie sheet, no less than 1/8 inch thick.

REMOVE wax paper.

SCORE with knife in whatever shapes you like.

SPRINKLE with seasoning or salt, if using.

PLACE in cold oven, HEAT oven to 300°, and BAKE 15 to 20
minutes or until lightly browned.

COOL 5 minutes, then REMOVE crackers from cookie sheet.

Hint: A food processor grinds seeds quite well.

Now these really taste like pretzels . . .

RYE PRETZELS

1 tablespoon dry yeast	4 to 4 1/2 cups rye flour
1 1/2 cups warm water	1 tablespoon caraway or
1 tablespoon molasses	sesame seeds
1 teaspoon salt	Coarse salt

PREHEAT oven to 425°.

GREASE cookie sheet.

DISSOLVE yeast in warm water.

ADD molasses and salt.

STIR in flour and seeds.

KNEAD in bowl for about 5 minutes.

CUT into 12 portions.

ROLL each portion into a rope about 15 inches long.

SHAPE into pretzels or any design you wish.

PLACE on greased cookie sheet.

DAB each pretzel lightly with a moistened cloth.

SPRINKLE with a little coarse salt.

BAKE at 425° for 20 minutes or until browned.

Yield: 12 pretzels

Nothing tastes as good as a fresh, homemade tortilla!

CORN TORTILLAS

2 cups Masa Harina corn meal (see note)
1 cup + additional water

COMBINE with hands until dough holds its shape.

ADD more water if necessary.

LET stand 15 minutes.

DIVIDE into 12 balls (about the size of golf balls).

DAMPEN dough slightly with water.

PRESS between sheets of wax paper with rolling pin.

ROLL to about 6 inches in diameter.

PLACE tortilla paper-side-up on ungreased griddle.

PEEL off paper and cook 30 seconds or until edges begin to dry.

TURN and COOK until surface appears puffy and dry.

SPREAD with butter, or FRY in hot oil.

STORE in refrigerator 2 weeks, or FREEZE.

REHEAT in oven or microwave.

Yield: 12 tortillas

Note: You can find this special corn meal in supermarkets near other corn meal.

Barley flour makes a great muffin. If you can tolerate gluten, experiment with cracked barley or barley flakes. If gluten is a problem, avoid barley.

ALL-BARLEY MUFFINS

2 cups barley flour
1 tablespoon baking powder
1 teaspoon salt
2 tablespoons granulated sugar

2 tablespoons cooking oil
1 cup water
2 eggs
1/2 cup raisins (optional)

PREHEAT oven to 425°.

GREASE muffin pans.

MIX flour, baking powder, salt, and sugar together well in large bowl.

BEAT oil, water, and eggs in another bowl until blended.

ADD to dry ingredients. ADD raisins, if using.

STIR only until dry ingredients are moistened.

SPOON batter into greased muffin pans until 3/4 full.

BAKE at 425° for 15 minutes or until browned.

Yield: about 12 muffins

Teff tastes a little like buckwheat. Nuts complement the taste.
If you have a problem with gluten, you may have to avoid teff.

TEFF MUFFINS

3/4 cup teff flour (see note)	1/4 teaspoon salt
3/4 cup rice flour	2 eggs
1/2 cup arrowroot (see note)	1/3 cup olive oil
1 1/2 teaspoons baking powder	2/3 cup water
1/2 teaspoon cinnamon	1/2 cup chopped filberts

PREHEAT oven to 400°.

GREASE muffins pans.

COMBINE flours, arrowroot, baking powder, cinamon, and salt.

MIX eggs, oil, and water, and ADD to the flour mixture,

MIXING quickly.

ADD nuts.

FILL greased muffin pans 3/4 full.

BAKE at 400° for 25 minutes.

Yield: 8 muffins

Note: You may substitute potato starch or tapioca flour for arrowroot.

Teff is a special grass grown as a cereal grain. It has been grown in Ethiopia for 4,000 years. Its iron content is almost three times higher than wheat's. Since 1985 it has been commercially grown in Idaho, and you can find it in health food stores.

Kathy Forsyth of Mt. Lebanon, Penn. shares this recipe.

CINNAMON RAISIN MUFFINS

4 cups medium rye flour
1/2 cup granulated sugar
8 teaspoons baking powder
1 teaspoon salt
2 cups dark seedless
  raisins

2 teaspoons cinnamon
8 tablespoons corn oil (see note)
2 cups water

PREHEAT oven to 375°.

GREASE muffin pans.

MIX flour, sugar, baking powders, salt, raisins, and cinnamon in medium bowl.

ADD corn oil and water, stirring until just moistened.

SPOON batter into muffin pans until 3/4 full.

BAKE at 375° for 30 to 35 minutes until muffins come away from edge of pan.

Yield: about 20 muffins

Note: You can use any cooking oil or even substitute applesauce for oil.

BLUEBERRY MUFFINS

2/3 cup banana (see note)
1 egg
1 cup milk or water
1/3 cup oil or shortening
2 teaspoons xanthan gum
2/3 cup potato flour or
    mashed potatoes

1 teaspoon soda
3 teaspoons baking powder
2/3 cup rice flour
2/3 cup bean flour
1 cup blueberries

PREHEAT oven to 300°.

OIL and FLOUR muffins pans.

MIX banana, egg, milk or water, and oil or shortening in processor.

SIFT dry ingredients. (MIX potato flour or potatoes very well.)

ADD flour mixture to egg mixture.

ADD blueberries.

FILL oiled and floured muffin pans 3/4 full.

BAKE at 300° for 40 minutes.

Yield: 12 muffins

Note: If you do not have a banana, 3 or 4 small canned yams plus 1/4 cup sugar equals 1 banana.

These muffins are my favorite! Delicious hot or cold.

APPLE OATMEAL MUFFINS

1 egg	*1 cup quick oats, uncooked*
3/4 cup wate	*1/3 cup granulated sugar*
1 cup raisins	*5 teaspoons baking powder*
1 chopped apple	*1 teaspoon salt*
1/2 cup oil	*1 teaspoon nutmeg*
7/8 cup rice flour	*2 teaspoons cinnamon*

PREHEAT oven to 375°.

GREASE muffins pans.

BEAT egg in large bowl.

STIR in remaining ingredients, mixing just to moisten.

POUR into greased muffin pans until almost full.

BAKE at 375° for 25 to 30 minutes.

Yield: 10 to 12 muffins

Very moist and flavorful!

CARROT BRAN MUFFINS

1 cup rice flour
1 1/2 cup millet or bean
  flour
1 1/2 tablespoons baking powder
1/2 teaspoon salt
1 tablespoon cinnamon
2 teaspoons xanthan gum
2 cups oat or rice bran

4 eggs
1 1/2 cups vegetable oil
1 1/4 cups dark brown
  sugar
1/4 cup molasses
3 cups finely grated
  carrots
1 cup raisins

PREHEAT oven to 325°.

GREASE muffin pans.

COMBINE flours, baking powder, salt, and xanthan gum.

ADD bran and SET ASIDE.

COMBINE in a separate bowl beaten eggs, oil, sugar, and molasses.

ADD carrots, raisins, and flour mixture, MIXING just to moisten.

FILL greased muffin pans nearly full.

BAKE at 325° for 30 minutes.

Yield: about 20 muffins

Mary Jane Stoneburg came to me in the Walnut Acres store in Penn's Creek, Penn., and handed me two beautiful orange muffins she had baked especially for me. Hope you will be as impressed as I was.

MJ'S ORANGE MUFFINS

1/4 cup oil
1/2 cup granulated sugar
2 eggs
1/4 cup frozen orange juice
   concentrate, thawed

1 cup water
1 1/2 cups + 1/2 cup rice flour
3 teaspoons baking powder
   (see note)
1/2 teaspoon salt

PREHEAT oven to 350°.

OIL muffins pans.

COMBINE oil, sugar, eggs, concentrate, water, and 1 1/2 cups rice flour in a processor or by stirring well.

MIX 1/2 cup rice flour, baking powder, and salt in another bowl.

ADD to egg mixture.

POUR immediately into oiled muffin pans until 3/4 full.

BAKE at 350° for 15 to 20 minutes.

Yield: 10 to 12 muffins

Note: Mary Jane cannot use baking powder and substitutes 1 1/2 teaspoons cream of tartar + 1 teaspoon baking soda. Either way the muffins come out very well.

She sometimes adds one of the following to the liquid:

1 cup blueberries
1 cup applesauce and 1/4 cup currants
2 ripe bananas
1 to 2 cups grated zucchini (omit the
   orange juice concentrate)
1 8-ounce can crushed pineapple +
   juice (which replaces 1/3 cup water.)

*If you really like MJ's muffins, you may appreciate
the convenience of a muffin mix.*

MUFFIN MIX

8 cups rice flour	*2 cups granulated sugar*
4 tablespoons baking powder	*2 teaspoons salt*

COMBINE all ingredients.

STORE for months in an airtight container, preferably in
refrigerator or freezer.

MJ'S MUFFINS FROM MIX

1/4 cup oil	*2 teaspoons ground cardamom*
2 eggs	*or 1/2 teaspoon anise seeds*
1/4 cup frozen orange juice	*or 2 tablespoons cocoa and*
concentrate, thawed	*2 teaspoons instant coffee*
1 cup water	*(optional)*
2 1/2 cups Muffin Mix	
(see recipe above)	

PREHEAT oven to 350°. GREASE muffins pans.

MIX oil, eggs, concentrate, and water.

ADD to muffin mix additional flavoring, if using.

ADD muffin mix to egg mixture and STIR well.

POUR immediately into greased muffin pans until 3/4 full.

BAKE at 350° for 15 to 20 minutes.

Yield: 10 to 12 muffins

See MJ's Orange Muffins recipe (above) for more optional ingredients
to add to your muffins.

The following two recipes use Muffin Mix.

POPPY SEED MUFFINS

1/4 cup oil	2 1/2 cups Muffin Mix (p. 57)
2 eggs	1/4 teaspoon nutmeg
1/4 cup frozen orange juice	1/2 cup golden raisins
concentrate, thawed	1/2 cup chopped pecans
1/2 teaspoon grated	6 tablespoons poppy seeds
orange peel	
1 cup water	

PREHEAT oven to 350°.

GREASE muffins pans.

MIX oil, eggs, concentrate, peel, and water in large bowl.

ADD muffin mix and STIR.

ADD remaining ingredients and STIR quickly until well mixed.

POUR immediately into greased muffin pans until 3/4 full.

BAKE at 350° for 20 to 25 minutes.

Yield: 10 to 12 muffins

These muffins really taste like bran muffins!

OAT-BRAN MUFFINS

1 cup quick oats, uncooked	1/2 cup cooking oil
1 cup boiling water	2 cups Muffin Mix (p. 57)
2 eggs, beaten	2 cups oat bran
1 1/2 cups water or fruit juice	1 teaspoon cinnamon
1/2 cup molasses	1 cup raisins

PREHEAT oven to 325°.

GREASE muffins pans.

MIX oats with boiling water and SET ASIDE to cool slightly.

MIX together eggs, water or juice, molasses, and oil.

ADD oatmeal mixture and COMBINE thoroughly.

MIX in another bowl muffin mix, bran, and cinnamon.

STIR in raisins.

ADD dry mixture to liquid and COMBINE.

SPOON mixture into greased muffin pans until 3/4 full.

BAKE at 325° for 30 minutes.

Yield: about 20 muffins

These muffins are made without the mix.

OAT-BRAN MUFFINS 2

1 cup quick oats, uncooked
1 cup boiling water
2 eggs, beaten
1 1/2 cups water or fruit juice
1/2 cup molasses
1/2 cup cooking oil
2 cups oat bran
3/4 cup rice flour

3/4 cup bean flour
1 teaspoon xanthan gum
1/2 cup brown sugar
2 teaspoons baking soda
1 teaspoon cinnamon
1/2 teaspoon salt
1 cup raisins

PREHEAT oven to 325°.

GREASE muffins pans.

MIX oats with boiling water and SET ASIDE to cool slightly.

MIX together eggs, water or juice, molasses, and oil.

ADD oatmeal mixture and MIX thoroughly.

MIX in another bowl bran, flours, xanthan gum, sugar, baking soda, cinnamon, and salt.

STIR in raisins.

ADD dry mixture to liquid and COMBINE.

SPOON mixture into greased muffin pans.

BAKE at 325° for 30 minutes.

Yield: about 18 muffins

A LOT OF TO-DO ABOUT BREAD MACHINES

I was never able to make a decent loaf of bread, and for most of my life there was no need to learn. But if, like me, you must avoid wheat or perhaps all grains, you will have good bread only if you make it yourself! So, the bread machine is a godsend. And yes, you can make wheat-free bread in a machine with very little effort. Here is what I have learned.

All bread machines use the same principles. The ingredients are combined, mixed, kneaded mechanically, and then baked, all in the same canister. There are many bread machines, but they seem to fall into two categories. One category contains machines in which you add dry yeast first, then dry ingredients, then liquid ingredients. You push a button and the machine does the rest. Both the small and large Welbilt work on this principle, for example.

The second category contains machines in which you add liquid ingredients first, then dry ingredients. Lastly, you sprinkle yeast over the top of the dry ingredients. Zojirushi, Panasonic, and the Hitachi machines work on this principle.

However, when you are using wheat-free recipes, you need to *change* this order. Mix all ingredients together *in a bowl* and *spoon* dough into the bread canister. Then, you push a button and the machine does its work. The dough is just too heavy to work well if you do not mix it first. You cannot use the feature that starts your bread making while you are away or asleep because the yeast will already be moistened, which means it will not rise.

To avoid disappointments, remember that you cannot interchange the methods used in the two categories.

If you wish to adapt your machine's recipes to wheat-free ones, be prepared for some trial and error loaves. *Sunset Magazine* (October 1993) had a comprehensive article, "How to Make Bread Machines Work for You" by Betsy Reynolds Bateson, from which I am quoting. "Recipes from general bread machine cookbooks are not usually developed for a particular machine and may work better in some machines than others." So you have some experimenting to do!

A few machines have a heat-up period before mixing, so you don't have to worry about temperature. But many machines require ingredients to be at room temperature, and some say that liquids need to be 75° to 110°. Yeast works best at 85°. Less than 75° slows the yeast's action; more than 120° will kill it.

"Machines can't compensate for variations in humidity, heat, altitude, and ingredients. That's why they sometimes produce overproofed loaves, loaves that don't rise properly, and loaves that are doughy—and why a recipe that's successful in spring and fall may not work as well in summer."

Keep track of the changes you make, so that next time you can build on your experience and keep track of what is working for you. Stay with your machine's flour capacity. One ingredient you will not need to change is the yeast. "If a loaf fails to work after you've experimented with the liquid and flour, you can change (one at a time) the other ingredients that affect rising . . . yeast, salt, sugar, and fat."

Keep yeast in the refrigerator and make sure it is still good. (See Getting Started, p. 3.)

"Salt retards yeast's action, so you may want to decrease it by half. Or, there might not be enough sugar to feed the yeast. Try increasing the sugar by 50%. If that doesn't work, reduce the fat—it also slows yeast's action."

I have heard it said that it is better to have a bread machine that has the mixer blade at the bottom of the canister because wheat-free dough tends to sit heavily on the bottom. You may want to experiment with the recipes that come with your machine, but the proportions of flour and liquid must be adjusted as in the recipes that follow.

On the following pages are listed some bread-making problems and possible solutions. *Try one suggestion at a time.* Take notes on what works and what doesn't. Thanks again to Betsy Reynolds Bateson for her October 1993 *Sunset Magazine* article.

BREAD MACHINE PROBLEMS

Problem 1

Sunken middle (flour-liquid ratio)
First, increase the flour by 2 tablespoons.
Next, decrease the sugar 1 teaspoon at a time.

Problem 2

Bread rises too high, then sinks (flour-liquid ratio)
First, decrease the liquid by 1 tablespoon.
Next, decrease the sugar by 50 percent
Next, decrease the yeast by 25 percent.
Next, decrease the fat by 50 percent.

Problem 3

Large uneven holes (leavening action too fast)
First, decrease the liquid 1 ounce at a time.
Next, decrease the yeast 1 teaspoon at a time.
Next, use regular active dry yeast rather than rapid or quick yeast.
Next, increase the salt by 50 percent.

Problem 4

Mountainous shape (too much flour)
First, reduce the flour.
Next, increase the yeast.
Next, increase the liquid, but not so much that recipe becomes too large for machine.

Problem 5

Too dense (inadequate gluten or inefficient leavening)
First, replace 1/4 to 1/2 cup flour with a finer flour, such as potato starch or tapioca flour.
Next, increase the yeast, or the sugar, or both.
Next, add 1 teaspoon liquid lecithin.
Next, pulverize a calcium tablet and add to batter.
Without gluten, eggs, or milk, most of your loaves will be dense, but they can still be tasty.

BREAD MACHINE RECIPES

Manna from heaven! Spelt is a grain used in biblical times. It is a variety of wheat some wheat-sensitive people can tolerate. You be the judge. If gluten is your problem, avoid spelt.

SPELT BREAD

1 tablespoon dried yeast
2 tablespoons granulated sugar
1/2 teaspoon salt
2 cups spelt flour
1 tablespoon oil
2 eggs
1 teaspoon cider or wine vinegar
Warm water

PLACE yeast and sugar together in one corner of canister (see note).

ADD salt and flour.

POUR oil, eggs, and vinegar in measuring cup.

GENTLY FILL cup with warm water to equal 1 cup + 2 tablespoons water.

ADD to bread canister. (Be sure kneader is in canister.)

SET controls to basic bread setting and PUSH start button.
You are free to diddle around for 2 hours and 15 minutes.

Note: If your bread machine requires liquid to be added first, combine all ingredients and mix in a bowl well, then add to your bread canister. You can also use your own manual bread-making skills (see p. 71).

*For the Zojirushi-type bread machine that makes
1 1/2-pound loaves.*

SPELT BREAD 2

1 1/2 tablespoons honey
1 1/2 tablespoons canola oil
1 cup + 2 tablespoons water
1 tablespoon yeast
3 cups spelt flour
1 teaspoon salt

COMBINE honey, oil, and water (see note).

ADD yeast, flour, and salt to the honey mixture.

PUT into bread canister. (Be sure kneader is in canister.)

SET machine to basic bread setting, PUSH start button, and you are free as a bird!

Note: If your bread machine requires yeast and dry ingredients to be added first, follow the directions on p. 61. You can also use your familiar manual bread-making skills (see p. 71).

Kamut (pronounced kah-mut) is another ancient grain. According to Arrowhead Mills, kamut flour "contains a unique type of gluten easier for your body to utilize than common wheat."

KAMUT BREAD

1 tablespoon yeast
3 cups kamut flour (see note)
1/2 teaspoon salt
1 1/2 tablespoons honey
1 1/2 tablespoons oil
1 cup + 6 tablespoons water

COMBINE yeast, flour, and salt in medium bowl.

COMBINE honey, oil, and water in large bowl.

ADD flour mixture to honey mixture and MIX well.

PUT into bread canister. (Be sure kneader is in canister.)

SET machine to basic setting, PUSH start button, and PUT your feet up!

If your bread machine requires yeast and dry ingredients to be added first, follow the directions on p. 61. You can also use your own manual bread making skills (see p. 71). However, cut back the liquid to 1 1/4 cups for each 3 cups flour.

Note: If you are gluten-intolerant, avoid kamut.

For the Welbilt-type bread machine that makes 1-pound loaves.

WALRUS BREAD

1 tablespoon yeast
2/3 cup garbanzo bean flour
   (see note)
1 cup rice flour
1/3 cup potato starch
1 1/2 tablespoons
   granulated sugar

1 teaspoon salt
2 teaspoons xanthan gum
1 tablespoon oil
1 teaspoon vinegar
1 egg
Warm water

PLACE yeast in one corner of bread canister bottom.

MIX remaining dry ingredients in large bowl.

ADD to canister. (Be sure kneader is in canister.)

COMBINE oil, vinegar, egg, and enough warm water to make 1 cup
+ 7 tablespoons liquid.

POUR over dry mixture.

SET controls for medium setting and PUSH start button.

CURL up with something you've been meaning to read!

Finished loaf should be 3 1/2 to 4 inches high.

Note: You may substitute 1 cup white bean flour, 1 cup corn flour, or
1 cup oat flour.

This recipe can be used for manual bread making (see p. 71). Follow
the directions in your own cookbooks.

For the Zojirushi-type bread machine that makes
1 1/2-pound loaves.

WALRUS BREAD 2

1 cup garbanzo bean flour
  (see note)
1 1/2 cups rice flour
1/2 cup potato starch
3 teaspoons xanthan gum
1 teaspoon salt
2 tablespoons
  granulated sugar

1 tablespoon yeast
2 eggs
2 tablespoons oil
1 teaspoon cider or
  wine vinegar
1 3/4 cups warm water
  (110° to 115°)

MIX dry ingredients in large bowl.

MIX eggs, oil, vinegar, and water in another bowl and ADD to the
dry mixture.

MIX until well moistened.

SPOON into canister. (Be sure kneader is in canister!)

SET controls for basic white bread at light setting and PUSH start
button.

CURL up with something you've been meaning to read!

Finished loaf should be about 5 inches high.

Note: You may substitute 1 cup white bean flour, 1 cup corn flour, or 1
cup oat flour, for garbanzo bean flour.

This recipe can be used for manual bread making (see p. 71). Follow
the directions in your own cookbooks.

After your basic bread recipe is the way you want it, vary the flavor with some of the following combinations.

SEASONING THE BREAD

For a 1 1/2-pound loaf try the following seasonings (see note):

1. *1 teaspoon celery flakes*
   1 teaspoon dried sage
   1/3 cup dried chopped onion

2. *1/2 teaspoon liquid lecithin*
   2 teaspoons caraway seeds
   1 teaspoon dried dill weed

3. *1 teaspoon vanilla extract*
   1/4 cup raisins
   1/4 cup dates
   1/4 cup walnuts
   1 teaspoon cinnamon

4. *1 teaspoon aniseed*
   1 teaspoon caraway
   Zest of 1 1/2 oranges, grated

5. *3 cups flour*
   3/4 cup liquid
   1/2 cup liquid egg substitute

6. *1/4 teaspoon fennel seed*
   1/2 teaspoon grated
    orange peel

7. *1/3 cup hulled millet*
   1/2 teaspoon liquid lecithin
   3/4 cup raw sunflower seeds

8. *3 tablespoons dried*
    chopped onion
   1 tablespoon caraway seeds

9. *1/4 teaspoon cardamon*
   1/4 cup chopped dates
   3 tablespoons chopped
    dried apricots
   1/3 cup chopped dried apples

10. *1 teaspoon cinnamon*
    Zest of 1 1/2 lemons, grated
    1 large egg OR 2 teaspoons
     liquid egg substitute

11. *3 tablespoons quinoa grain*
    1/3 cup sesame seeds

12. *1/4 cup dried chopped*
     onion

Note: For 1-pound loaves, use 2/3 of these quantities.

MANUAL BREAD MAKING

Dough for a bread machine tends to be sticky, like a very heavy batter. But you can still use bread machine recipes to make bread manually. Just add enough extra flour to make the dough easy to work with. Experiment by sprinkling dough and hands with flour until they are no longer sticky.

After you have kneaded the dough for a few minutes and it is soft and silky smooth but *not* sticky, it is ready for its first rising.

When a recipe instructs you to knead dough for 1 minute after the first rising period, but before forming it, *do not* add flour. Knead dough in its bowl. What you are doing is moving the sweetener around so the yeast has a new food source.

If your recipe asks you to oil the top of the dough before rising, do it gently with your fingertips.

Most recipes will tell you to let the dough rise until it is double in bulk. A wheat-free loaf will not double in size, but more likely it will rise to half again its bulk. Experience will tell how long that will take, but it is usually a little longer than with wheat flour. When it has risen to half again, it is ready to be punched down. Then go on to the next step.

When you shape the loaf for the second rising, handle it gently.

When the bread is done baking, it should sound hollow when you tap it with your fingers or a knife. If you are like me, you will be wondering what "hollow" sounds like or if it sounds hollow enough. Experience, they tell me, is the best teacher in this case!

Helpful Hints

If it is difficult to find a warm place for the dough to rise, consider putting the bowl on a heating pad turned to the low setting. The ideal temperature for yeast to multiply is 82° to 85°.

Immediately remove baked loaves from pans and lay loaves on their sides on wire racks to cool. Fresh bread slices better when cool, unless you are using an electric knife. When cool, slice unused portions, package tightly, label, and freeze. If you are rotating your foods, labeling is especially important.

You can do many good things with your "not so successful" bread experiments. Save leftovers for recipes like Stewed Bread (p. 135) or to make stuffing for turkey.

Barley flour makes great bread, but if gluten is a problem, avoid it.

BARLEY BREAD

1 tablespoon yeast
2 teaspoons brown sugar,
  divided
1 cup warm water, divided

2 cups barley flour, divided
1 tablespoon oil
1 teaspoon salt
1/3 cup bean flour

PREHEAT oven to 350°.

GREASE cookie sheet.

PUT yeast into small bowl.

ADD 1/2 teaspoon sugar and 1/2 cup water.

PUT in a warm place to rise.

PUT remaining 1/2 cup water into large mixing bowl.

ADD 1 cup barley flour and MIX vigorously.

ADD remaining 1 1/2 teaspoons brown sugar, oil, and salt and
MIX well.

ADD softened yeast and BEAT briskly,

ADD bean flour and enough remaining barley flour to make dough
that can be kneaded.

PLACE on floured board and KNEAD until smooth and elastic.

SHAPE into two round loaves on greased cookie sheet and SLASH
diagonally across tops.

LET RISE until double in bulk.

OIL tops lightly, if desired, for more crispness.

BAKE at 350° for 1 hour.

REMOVE from pans onto wire rack and COOL.

Bud and Jean Clem contributed this excellent bread recipe.

*For bread machines that make 1 1/2-pound loaves, here's a
flavorful rye bread. This recipe should work for any machine
which specifies adding liquids first and dry ingredients last.*

HIGH FIVE RYE BREAD

2 to 3 tablespoons honey
1 3/4 cups lukewarm water
1 tablespoon canola oil
2 teaspoons cider or
   wine vinegar
1 cup brown rice flour
1 1/2 cups rye flour
1 cup oat flour
1 teaspoon xanthan gum
1 teaspoon sea salt

1 tablespoon + 1 teaspoon yeast
2 teaspoons cinnamon
1/2 teaspoon anise seeds
2 teaspoons instant coffee
   granules
2 tablespoons cocoa
2 tablespoons caraway seeds
   (optional)
1/2 cup raisins (optional)

COMBINE honey, water, oil, and vinegar and SET ASIDE.
COMBINE flours, xanthan gum, salt, yeast, cinnamon, anise, coffee,
and cocoa. ADD liquid ingredients to dry ingredients and MIX well.
SPOON into bread canister. (Be sure kneader is in canister)
ADD raisins and caraway, if using, when bread machine indicates.
BAKE at longest cycle or at basic white bread, medium cycle. (If
your machine cannot bake long enough to bake the bread completely,
next time try baking it in a preheated conventional oven at 300° for 2
hours.)
PUT your feet up with a good book . . . or just watch the grass grow!
TURN loaf out of canister when done and COOL on wire rack
before slicing.

SOURDOUGH GUIDELINES

Guidelines for Maintaining a Sweet Spirit Whilst Working with Sourdough

Researching the subject of sourdough baking is like climbing a mountain—only everybody is climbing a different mountain! Because there are so many ways to make starter, "feed" it, and use it, I will use the easiest way—certainly not the only way.

Because everyone measures a little differently, everyone's sourdough starter will be slightly different. And humidity changes from day to day, so you can see that success may be illusive. Keep track of what you do (if this is your book, you can write in it!) and experiment with the amount of liquid you add to your batter.

If you want to experiment without using sourdough, remember that the sourdough starter is 1 cup water and 1 cup flour. Adjust your recipe accordingly.

Equipment You Need

Start with a jar or crock that will hold at least 1/2 gallon liquid. You can cover it with cloth or plastic or a pottery lid; just be sure you do not let the contents come in contact with metal.

Making Sourdough Starter

TEST your yeast by adding a pinch of granulated sugar and 1 teaspoon warm water to about 1 tablespoon starter. If it bubbles and foams, it is working.

ADD the following to your jar:

*2 cups warm water (no more than 115° for dried yeast
   or 90° for yeast cake)*
1 tablespoon dry powdered yeast or 1 yeast cake
2 cups rice flour
1 teaspoon granulated sugar

ALLOW mixture to sit at room temperature until fermented and
bubbly—about 15 minutes in a warm room.
COVER and REFRIGERATE when bubbly and slightly risen.
WAIT at least 24 hours before using.

Note: Some say starter should always be refrigerated. Others say to
keep starter at room temperature 5 days, stirring each morning, and
on day 6 begin using, then refrigerate. Still others say to let the starter
stand in a warm position for 30 minutes, then store in the fridge until
needed. I think what you do depends on just how sour you like your
baked goods. The longer the starter stands on your counter, the
stronger the sour taste.

Note: Dr. Green encourages the use of natural "wild" yeasts, but I
have not worked with them.

Your Schedule

Day 1   PUT your starter ingredients together and cover.
Days 2, 3, 4   STIR with a wooden spoon.
Day 5   FEED the starter

            1 cup flour
            1 cup warm water
            1 teaspoon granulated sugar

COVER loosely with cloth or plastic. LET REST for 24 hours.

Day 6   TAKE OUT the amount you need for your recipe.

Always have the starter at room temperature before using. Most sourdough baking failures occur because the basic starter was kept too cool the night before baking or was refrigerated and wasn't at room temperature.

Replace whatever quantity you've taken by using the same recipe you used to feed the starter.

If starter becomes too sour, simply add a pinch of baking soda to sweeten it.

If starter becomes dry, bring it back to life with water, warmth, and a teaspoon of sweetener (sugar, honey, or fructose).

It might be fun to try an . . .

OLD FASHIONED STARTER

1 large potato boiled in 1 pint water until mushy
1 tablespoon dry yeast or 1 yeast cake
1/4 cup granulated sugar

MASH potato well.

POUR potato, yeast, and sugar into quart jar.

KEEP at room temperature until bubbling and lively.

COVER and REFRIGERATE.

USE same as you use sourdough starter.

This is a revised traditional recipe adapted from the
Small Farm Journal, *Winter 1991.*

AMISH FRIENDSHIP BREAD

1 cup Sourdough Starter   *7/8 cup bean flour*
  (p. 75)   *1 cup granulated sugar*
2/3 cup oil   *1 teaspoon cinnamon*
3 eggs   *2 teaspoons baking powder*
1 teaspoon vanilla   *1/2 teaspoon baking soda*
1 cup rice flour   *1/2 teaspoon salt*

Optional: *1/4 cup chopped citron*
              or 1/4 cup chopped glacéd cherries
              or 1/2 cup raisins
              or 1/2 cup chopped nuts
              or whatever suits your pleasure!

PREHEAT oven to 300°.

GREASE and FLOUR medium loaf pan.

MIX liquid ingredients in large bowl and SET ASIDE.

MIX dry ingredients in separate bowl.

ADD any optional ingredients to dry ingredients, COATING them well.

ADD to liquid ingredients.

POUR into greased and floured loaf pan.

BAKE at 300° for 60 minutes.

These pancakes are so easy to make when you're camping and are so good, you don't even have to tell anyone they're wheat-free.

SOURDOUGH PANCAKES

3 cups Sourdough Starter
  (p. 75)
2 tablespoons granulated
  sugar or honey
1/4 teaspoon salt

1 egg, well beaten
1 tablespoon cooking oil
Wheat-free flour as needed
1 teaspoon baking soda
2 tablespoons warm water

MIX together starter, sugar or honey, salt, egg, and oil.

ADD 1/4 to 1/2 cup any wheat-free flour, if batter is too thin.

ADD baking soda and warm water just before baking. Batter should foam up immediately.

DROP by 1/4 cupfuls onto oiled hot griddle.

COOK 2 to 3 minutes each side.

SERVE hot with your favorite toppings.

Yield: 10 to 12 pancakes

This sourdough bread recipe is for manual bread making.

SOURDOUGH BREAD

*1 cup Sourdough Starter
  (p. 75)
2 cups warm water
2 tablespoons honey
2 teaspoons salt*

*2 tablespoons cooking oil
2 cups rice flour
2 cups bean flour
4 teaspoons xanthan gum
1 tablespoon yeast*

TAKE starter out the night before to bring to room temperature.
MIX together starter, water, honey, salt, and oil.
ADD flours and xanthan gum and MIX well. If dough is sticky,
FLOUR your hands. Try not to add too much flour to the dough.
COVER dough and LET RISE about 4 hours or until almost doubled.
PREHEAT oven to 300°.
GREASE 2 loaf pans or a cookie sheet.
SHAPE dough into 2 loaves, kneading just a little.
PUT into greased loaf pans or on cookie sheet for a French loaf.
LET RISE for 2 hours until about doubled.
BAKE at 300° for 60 minutes.

For the Welbilt-type bread machine that makes 1-pound loaves or any machine that specifies dry ingredients first and liquids last.

SOURDOUGH BREAD 2

1 teaspoon yeast
1 cup rice flour
1 cup bean flour
2 teaspoons xanthan gum
1 teaspoon salt
1 1/2 tablespoons granulated
* sugar or 1 tablespoon honey*

1/2 cup Sourdough Starter
* (p. 75)*
1 cup + 1 tablespoon
* warm water*
1 tablespoon oil

TAKE starter out the night before to bring to room temperature.

PLACE yeast in corner of canister bottom.

MIX flours, xanthan gum, salt and sugar or honey.

ADD to canister. (Be sure kneader is in canister.)

COMBINE starter, water, and oil, and ADD to canister.

SET controls for dark setting.

PUT your feet up and write your best friend a letter!

For the Zoshirushi-type bread machine that makes
1 1/2 pound loaves OR any machine that specifies adding
liquids first and dry ingredients last.

SOURDOUGH BREAD 3

1 tablespoon
+ 1/2 teaspoon yeast
1 1/2 cups rice flour
1 cup bean flour
1/2 cup potato starch
3 teaspoons xanthan gum
1 teaspoon salt

2 tablespoons sugar
or 1 1/2 tablespoons honey
3/4 cup Sourdough Starter
(p. 75)
1 tablespoon oil
About 1 1/2 cups warm
water

TAKE starter out the night before to bring to room temperature.

MIX dry ingredients together.

MIX starter, oil, and enough water in large measuring cup to make 2 cups liquid.

ADD liquid ingredients to dry ingredients and MIX well.

PUT into canister. (Be sure kneader is in canister.)

SET controls for French bread setting, a longer setting good for sourdough bread.

PUT up your feet and think good things about yourself!

BAGELS

We have to talk about bagels.

Most of my failures with bagels came about, I believe, because they need a long rising time and I was judging them by wheat standards. So leave them alone and be patient.

This is how I made great bagels: I punched down the dough after 3 hours and put the covered bowl in the refrigerator. Next morning I formed the bagels, covered them, and left them in a cool kitchen until I came home at noon, at which time I placed them on a warm heating pad and went about my business. By about 3 o'clock they had risen about 1/2 inch, so I proceeded with the boiling process, and then the baking. . . .

Husband Ed and I, armed with a small bag of bagels baked for 40 minutes and another baked for 50 minutes, sampled all the way to an auction.

"Hand me another of the 50-minute bagels," says Ed.

"I like the 40-minute bagels," I reply.

"Too chewy," he says. "But not bad. Hand me one of those, too."

The upshot is that we could not decide, so that decision is left to you!

Bagels dry out quickly, so warm or toast them after a day or two.

SOURDOUGH BAGELS

2 cups Sourdough Starter (p. 75)	1 tablespoon yeast
2 cups rice flour	3 tablespoons oil
2 cups bean flour	1/2 cup warm water
4 teaspoons xanthan gum	2 tablespoons honey
1 teaspoon salt	1 egg (optional)

Glaze:

1 egg white + 1 tablespoon cold water

COMBINE flours, xanthan gum, salt, and yeast and MIX well.

ADD remaining ingredients. KNEAD until smooth and elastic.

PLACE in oiled bowl. COVER.

LET RISE for 3 hours in a warm place (a heating pad helps).

KNEAD again, gently, and ROLL to 1/2 to 3/4 inches thick. Try not to roll out too many times; the dough absorbs more flour each time and will get heavier.

CUT out or FORM bagel shapes on lightly floured board. (I used a pineapple cutter!)

LET RISE about 2 hours or until you see about 1/2-inch increase in height of dough.

BOIL about 2 inches water in a large pan.

ADD about 3 bagels at a time and SIMMER 6 minutes.

TURN over bagels and SIMMER about 1 more minute.

REMOVE from water and PLACE on towel or cloth. COOL 5 minutes.

PREHEAT oven to 350°.

PLACE on ungreased cookie sheets. BRUSH tops with oil or glaze.

BAKE at 350° for 40 to 50 minutes. (See comments preceding recipe.)

Main Courses

COME YE THANKFUL PEOPLE
COME RAISE THE SONG OF HARVEST-HOME:
ALL IS SAFELY GATHERED IN
ERE THE WINTER STORMS BEGIN.

—Henry Alford (1810-1871)

FAME IS AT BEST AN UNPERFORMING CHEAT;
BUT 'TIS SUBSTANTIAL HAPPINESS TO EAT.

—Alexander Pope

Corn flour (not to be confused with cornstarch) is great for pan frying. Corn meal works, but corn flour gets crisper.

CRISPY FRIED CHICKEN

1 cup corn flour
2 teaspoons salt
1/2 teaspoon garlic salt
1/4 teaspoon pepper
1 egg, slightly beaten

1 tablespoon water
2 3-pound frying chickens,
*   washed and quartered*
Shortening or cooking oil

COMBINE corn flour, salt, garlic salt, and pepper in a brown bag.
SHAKE thoroughly.
COMBINE egg and water on a plate.
DIP chicken pieces in egg mixture.
SHAKE each piece in bag until coated.
PAIR oil in large frying pan about 1/2-inch deep.
FRY and TURN pieces at medium high heat until golden brown on all sides.
REDUCE heat, COVER, and COOK about 40 minutes or until tender.
UNCOVER for the last 10 minutes for crisper chicken.

Yield: 8 servings

SWEET AND SOUR CHICKEN

2 to 3 pounds chicken, washed and cut up
1 8-ounce jar apricot preserves
1 package onion soup mix
1 8-ounce jar Thousand Island dressing

PREHEAT oven to 350°.

PLACE chicken pieces in a baking dish in one layer.

SPOON apricot preserves on each piece.

SPRINKLE with onion soup mix.

POUR dressing over each piece.

COVER and BAKE at 350° for 1 1/2 hours.

Yield: 4 servings

ORANGE CHICKEN

1 6-ounce can frozen orange
  juice concentrate, thawed
6 ounces water
1/4 cup dark brown sugar
1 medium onion (about 2/3 cup)

1 teaspoon oregano
1/2 teaspoon nutmeg
Cooked chicken pieces from
  1 medium fryer (boiled and
  drained, baked, or fried)

MIX all ingredients.

HEAT in covered frying pan at medium heat 30 minutes or until warm.

Yield: 4 servings

BARBEQUED HAWAIIAN CHICKEN

1 fryer, washed and cut up
1/4 cup apricot preserves
1/4 cup Russian salad dressing
2 tablespoons dry onion soup mix

MICROWAVE chicken parts, covered, on high for 15 minutes,
TURNING dish every 3 minutes.

GRILL over hot coals for 5 minutes.

COMBINE remaining ingredients and BRUSH over chicken.

GRILL 10 more minutes or until done.

CHICKEN PIE

1 Double Pie Crust, unbaked (p. 152), divided
1 small boiled chicken, boned and cut up
2 egg yolks
1/2 cup sweet or sour cream or chicken stock
1 cup peas or other vegetable, chopped (optional)

PREHEAT oven to 325°.

ROLL out 1/2 pastry dough and LINE pie pan or baking dish.

FILL with chicken and vegetables, if using.

MIX egg yolks and cream or stock, and POUR into pan.

ROLL OUT rest of pastry and COVER pan with it.

BAKE at 325° for 1/2 to 1 hour until browned.

Here's something special!

CLUCKING PEAR STIR-FRY

3/4 cup cold water	1/4 cup sliced almonds
3 tablespoons frozen orange juice concentrate	1 tablespoon cooking oil
	1 4-ounce can mushrooms
2 tablespoons tamari	2 medium sweet peppers, sliced
2 teaspoons cornstarch	2 medium unpeeled pears, sliced
1/4 teaspoon ginger	12 ounces skinless, boneless
1/4 teaspoon cinnamon	chicken in 1-inch pieces
Dash cayenne pepper	Hot cooked brown rice for 4

COMBINE water, orange juice, tamari, cornstarch, ginger, cinnamon, and cayenne pepper and SET ASIDE.

PREHEAT skillet or wok over medium high heat.

STIR-FRY almonds 1 minute to toast and REMOVE from pan.

STIR-FRY mushrooms, peppers, and pears in oil until crisp-tender and REMOVE from pan.

ADD chicken and COOK 3 minutes or until tender.

PUSH chicken to side of pan.

ADD orange juice mixture and COOK until thickened.

STIR in chicken and pear mixture and HEAT.

ADD almonds.

SERVE over rice.

Yield: 4 servings

SAVORY STUFFING WITH OYSTERS

1 cup chopped celery
1 cup chopped onion
   (optional)
1/2 cup butter or margarine
1 bay leaf
12 cups dry leftover bread
   cubes

2 to 3 jars raw oysters
2 teaspoons poultry seasoning
   or 1 teaspoon EACH
   basil, thyme, sage,
   and celery seed
Salt and pepper to taste
2 eggs, beaten

MIX together all ingredients.

STUFF turkey cavities before roasting bird.

LET SET 5 minutes before serving.

Yield: enough for a 20-pound turkey

CINNAMON RAISIN STUFFING

5 tablespoons butter
1 large onion, coarsely
  chopped
6 ounces dried apple slices
1/2 teaspoon dried sage

3 cups day-old wheat-free
  bread (or any sweet bread)
  cut into 1-inch cubes
1 teaspoon cinnamon
1/3 cup raisins

HEAT butter in saucepan.

ADD onion and SAUTE until tender, about 6 minutes.

STIR in apple slices, sage, and bread cubes. MIX well.

PRUNE APPLE STUFFING

4 tablespoons bacon fat
  (or other shortening)
2 cups diced tart apples
  (unpeeled)
1 cup prunes
1/2 cup dry wheat-free
  bread crumbs

1 teaspoon tarragon
1 teaspoon rosemary
1 teaspoon dried parsley
Salt, nutmeg, cinnamon to
  taste

PUT shortening, apples, and prunes in a saucepan.

COOK for 5 minutes.

ADD remaining ingredients and MIX well.

STUFF in duck or goose cavities.

Yield: 2 cups

Use 8 cups stuffing for a 10-pound turkey.

ROAST TURKEY WITH STUFFING

THAW frozen turkey before stuffing.

PREPARE Savory Stuffing or Cinnamon Raisin Stuffing (see recipes opposite page).

PREHEAT oven to 325°.

RINSE bird thoroughly inside and out. STUFF both cavities of turkey.

TRUSS by tying legs close to the body and firmly to the tail.

SEW stuffed cavities closed or FASTEN with skewers and LACE with string.

PLACE breast side up on rack in open roasting pan.

RUB skin with butter or cooking oil.

COVER bird loosely with aluminum foil. Do not let foil touch the heating element in an electric oven.

ROAST at 325° until tender. Use the following chart:

Weight (pounds)	Hours
4 to 6	3 to 4
8 to 12	4 to 4 1/2
12 to 16	4 1/2 to 5
16 to 20	6 to 8
20 to 24	8 to 9

Half an hour before end of roasting time, TURN BACK foil so skin can brown. Meat thermometer will register 190°.

LET STAND 20 minutes when done, to facilitate carving.

An easier way is to PLACE prepared turkey in a roasting bag, which produces a juicy product in less time, without the cleanup.

FOLLOW directions on the box.

ROAST GOOSE

THAW goose, if frozen.

REMOVE neck, giblets, and loose fat.

SIMMER neck and giblets for gravy.

MIX and BAKE stuffing in a separate pan (see stuffing recipes p. 91 or p. 92).

PREHEAT oven to 400°.

PUT slice of onion and 1 or 2 celery sticks in cavity.

PLACE goose on rack in roasting pan.

COVER with tight-fitting lid so steam and juices remain.

OR

USE a roasting bag for speedier cooking with very little mess.

FOLLOW directions on box.

ROAST at 400°. USE the following chart:

Weight (pounds)	Hours
5 to 7	3/4 to 2
7 to 9	2 to 2 1/4
9 to 11	2 1/2 to 2 3/4

When done, REMOVE cover for 10 minutes to brown skin.

Meat thermometer will register 185°.

To go with the goose:

CORE red apples but do not peel.

CUT into 1/4-inch-thick slices.

FRY in butter until lightly browned.

DRAIN and SPRINKLE with sugar.

ROAST WILD DUCK

1/2 cup chicken broth
1 6-ounce can frozen orange juice concentrate, thawed
1 orange, sliced

PREHEAT oven to 225°.

STUFF duck with prune apple stuffing (see p. 92), mixed with
> *1 teaspoon tarragon*
> *1 teaspoon rosemary*
> *1 teaspoon parsley*

MIX broth, concentrate, and orange and PUT in roasting bag with duck.

ROAST in bag at 225° for 5 to 6 hours.

PERSIAN LAMB WITH PEACHES

1 pound peaches, nectarines, or pears or
  a 1-pound can sliced peaches, drained
Lemon juice
2 pounds lean boneless lamb shoulder
1 teaspoon cinnamon
1/2 teaspoon cloves
1/4 teaspoon pepper
2 tablespoons brown sugar
1 medium onion, chopped
2 tablespoons lemon juice
4 teaspoons EACH cornstarch and water
Salt
Hot cooked rice for 4 to 6 servings
Fresh mint leaves
Plain yogurt (optional)

PEEL and slice fruit.

SPRINKLE with lemon juice (omit for canned peaches) and
SET ASIDE.

TRIM excess fat from lamb and CUT meat into 3/4-inch cubes.

ARRANGE cubes in microwavable shallow 2-quart baking dish.

MIX together in a small bowl cinnamon, cloves, pepper, and sugar.

SPRINKLE over lamb.

ADD onion and lemon juice.

COVER with lid or plastic wrap.

MICROWAVE on high for 5 minutes; STIR well.

MICROWAVE covered on medium for 30 minutes, STIRRING after 15 minutes or until meat is fork-tender.

LET STAND 5 minutes.

TRANSFER lamb cubes with slotted spoon to plate and COVER.

STIR cornstarch into water until dissolved.

STIR into lamb juices.

MICROWAVE uncovered on high for 2 to 3 minutes, STIRRING each minute until bubbly and thickened.

STIR in meat. SPOON over rice.

GARNISH with peaches and mint.

PASS yogurt, if using

Yield: 4 to 6 servings

BAKED HAM

Fully cooked ham
1 cup Ham Glaze (see p. 302)

PREHEAT oven to 275°.

FOLLOW directions on label for fully cooked ham.

PLACE ham face down on baking pan.

COVER pan securely with foil.

BAKE at 275° for 10 minutes per pound.

REMOVE pan from oven 30 minutes before baking time is up.

REMOVE drippings from pan.

RETURN uncovered ham to oven.

BRUSH on ham glaze (see p. HMG) frequently during the last 30 minutes of baking. A basting brush is helpful.

REMOVE ham from oven and SERVE.

THANKSGIVING VEGETABLES

2 pints brussels sprouts	1/2 cup apple cider
24 white pearl onions	1/2 cup honey or maple syrup
20 ounces preserved	2 tablespoons butter or margarine
kumquats	2 teaspoons dried thyme
2 to 3 large semiripe pears,	1/4 teaspoon freshly ground pepper
peeled, cored, quartered	1 tablespoon chopped fresh mint

CUT thin slice off bottom of each sprout, and CUT an X on bottom.

PLACE sprouts in boiling water and BLANCH 5 minutes.

DRAIN, RUN under cold water, PAT dry, and SET ASIDE.

COOK onions in boiling water 7 minutes.

DRAIN, RUN under cold water, and PAT dry.

SLICE roots off whole onions and SET ASIDE.

DRAIN kumquats, RINSE, and RESERVE.

CUT pear quarters lengthwise into 1/4-inch slices.

PREHEAT oven to 350°.

HEAT cider, honey or syrup, butter or margarine, and thyme in small saucepan until butter melts, STIRRING occasionally.

LAY vegetables in 4 rows crosswise in a 9 x 13 x 2-inch ovenproof dish.

POUR cider mixture over vegetables and SPRINKLE with black pepper.

COVER dish with aluminum foil.

BAKE for 45 minutes, BASTING twice.

UNCOVER and BAKE for 15 more minutes until vegetables are glazed and browned on top.

BASTE before serving. SPRINKLE with mint.

Yield: 12 servings

MEAT BALLS STROGANOFF

1 pound hamburger	1 tablespoon margarine
1/2 cup oatmeal or	1/2 pound mushrooms, sliced
bread crumbs	1/2 cup chopped onion
1/2 cup water	2 tablespoons rice flour
1 1/4 teaspoons salt, divided	1 cup condensed beef bouillon
1/2 teaspoon pepper, divided	1 teaspoon Worcestershire sauce
3 tablespoons oil	1/4 cup non-dairy sour cream

COMBINE hamburger, oatmeal or bread crumbs, water, 1 teaspoon salt, and 1/4 teaspoon pepper in large skillet.

FORM into 1-inch balls.

HEAT oil in skillet at medium high heat.

BROWN meatballs on oil, then REMOVE from pan.

SAUTE margarine, mushrooms, and onion 10 minutes in same pan.

ADD flour and MIX.

STIR in bouillon.

ADD meat balls, Worcestershire sauce, 1/4 teaspoon salt, and 1/4 teaspoon pepper.

COVER and SIMMER 20 minutes.

MIX in sour cream.

SERVE over noodles (p. 44).

So easy and so good!

IMPOSSIBLE BACON QUICHE

12 slices (1/2 pound) bacon, fried and crumbled
1 cup (4 ounces) Swiss cheese, shredded
1/3 cup finely chopped onion
2 cups milk or water
1/2 cup Biscuit Mix (p. 14)
4 eggs
Salt and pepper to taste

PREHEAT oven to 350°.

GREASE 9 or 10-inch pie pan.

SPRINKLE bacon, cheese, and onion over bottom of pan.

BLEND for 1 minute milk or water, biscuit mix, eggs, salt, and pepper.

POUR into greased pan.

BAKE for 50 to 55 minutes or until knife inserted in center comes
out clean.

LET stand 5 minutes.

IMPOSSIBLE PIZZA PIE

2/3 cup chopped onion
1/3 cup grated Parmesan cheese
3 eggs

1 1/2 cups milk or water
3/4 cup Biscuit Mix (p. 14)

Sauce:

1 6-ounce can tomato paste
1/4 cup water
1 teaspoon oregano

1/2 teaspoon garlic salt
1/2 teaspoon basil
1/4 teaspoon pepper

Topping:

1/4 cup grated Parmesan cheese
3 1/2 ounces pepperoni, sliced
1/3 cup chopped onion
1/2 cup chopped green pepper
1 cup shredded mozzarella cheese

PREHEAT oven to 425°.

GREASE 10-inch pie pan.

SPRINKLE onion and cheese in pan.

BEAT eggs, milk or water, and biscuit mix until smooth, 15 seconds
in processor on high or 1 minute by hand.

POUR into pan.

BAKE 20 minutes.

SPREAD sauce over top.

LAYER topping ingredients on sauce.

BAKE until cheese is light brown, 15 to 20 minutes.

COOL 5 minutes.

Yield: 6 to 8 servings

My favorite . . .

IMPOSSIBLE HAM AND SWISS PIE

2 cups fully cooked ham chunks
1 cup (4 ounces) shredded natural Swiss cheese
1/3 cup chopped green or regular onions
1/4 teaspoon salt
1/8 teaspoon pepper
1 cup Biscuit Mix (p. 14)
2 cups milk or water
4 eggs

PREHEAT oven to 400°.

GREASE 10-inch pie pan.

SPRINKLE ham, cheese, and onions in pan.

BEAT remaining ingredients until smooth, 15 seconds in processor
on high or 1 minute by hand.

POUR into pan.

BAKE until golden brown and knife inserted in center comes out
clean, 35 to 40 minutes.

COOL 5 minutes.

Yield: 6 servings

IMPOSSIBLE CHEESEBURGER PIE

1 pound ground beef
1 1/2 cups chopped onion
1 1/2 cups milk or water
3 eggs
3/4 cup Biscuit Mix (p. 14)

1/4 teaspoon pepper
1/2 teaspoon salt
2 sliced tomatoes
1 cup grated cheddar cheese

PREHEAT oven to 400°.

GREASE 10-inch pie pan.

BROWN beef and onion, DRAIN, and SPREAD in greased pie pan.

BEAT milk or water, eggs, biscuit mix, pepper, and salt for 15 seconds in processor on high or 1 minute by hand.

POUR over hamburger.

BAKE at 400° for 25 minutes.

TOP with sliced tomatoes and cheese.

BAKE 5 to 8 minutes more or until knife inserted in center comes out clean.

POLISH LENTIL STEW

2 cups water
2 beef bouillon cubes or
   2 teaspoons broth granules
1 cup dried lentils, rinsed
8 ounces Polish sausage, sliced
1 cup sliced celery
1 cup chopped onions
1 16-ounce can pureed tomatoes
1 clove garlic, minced

BOIL water and bouillon in 4-quart Dutch oven.

ADD lentils, sausage, celery, onions, tomatoes, and garlic.

BOIL and STIR for 1 minute.

REDUCE heat, COVER, leaving cover ajar, and SIMMER 45 to 50 minutes.

ADD water if too thick.

Yield: 4 servings

CHEESE ENCHILADAS

12 corn tortillas
Red Chili Sauce (p. 299)
1 pound mild cheddar or longhorn
  cheese, grated
1 medium onion, chopped
Black olives, chopped

DIP tortillas one at a time in chili sauce for just a second to soften.

STACK on a plate ready to use.

PREHEAT oven to 400°.

PLACE handful of cheese in middle of each tortilla, reserving 1/2 cup for topping.

ROLL up with end tucked under and PLACE in 9 x 12-inch baking dish.

COVER with chili sauce.

SPRINKLE cheese on top.

BAKE at 400° for 20 minutes.

A family favorite, especially with homemade tortillas . . .

CHILI STACKS

1 pound hamburger	*1/4 teaspoon basil*
1/2 cup chopped onion	*1 15-ounce can tomato sauce*
1 teaspoon salt	*5 corn tortillas*
1 tablespoon chili powder	*1 cup grated jack or*
1/2 teaspoon oregano	*cheddar cheese*

BROWN hamburger and onion.

ADD salt, chili powder, oregano, basil, and tomato sauce.

SIMMER 10 minutes.

PREHEAT oven to 350°.

LAYER tortillas, sauce, mixture, and cheese (ending with sauce and cheese) in shallow baking dish.

BAKE at 350° for 15 minutes or until cheese melts.

Yield: 10 wedges

CHILES RELLENOS

For each relleno:
1 egg
1/2 teaspoon baking powder
1 canned cheese-stuffed whole peeled green chiles

PROCESS or blend egg and baking powder 60 seconds or until batter is foamy.

POUR into 4- to 5-inch circle in hot buttered skillet or griddle.

PLACE chile on one side of batter and FOLD over the other side like an omelet.

COOK for several minutes until golden brown on each side and cheese is melted.

SERVE immediately with Green Chili Sauce (p. 300).

Dottie Force served this at a square dance. She said a salad and chips make this a good meal.

SKILLET TAMALE PIE

1 pound ground beef	1 15-ounce can stewed tomatoes
1 teaspoon salt	Dash lemon pepper
1/2 teaspoon poultry seasoning	1 tablespoon chili powder
1 cup chopped onion	1 cup corn meal
1 cup chopped green pepper	1 cup sour cream or tofu
1 15-ounce can whole kernel corn, undrained	1 cup grated jack or cheddar cheese

MIX and cook beef, salt, and poultry seasoning. DRAIN.

ADD onion, green pepper, corn, tomatoes, lemon pepper, and chili powder in large skillet and HEAT to boiling.

ADD chili, corn meal, and sour cream or tofu and STIR well.

COOK a few minutes to thicken.

SPRINKLE cheese on top and LET MELT.

Yield: 6 to 8 servings

A very filling spoonbread style vegetable dish . . .
Be sure to chop veggies finely.

MEXICAN VEGETABLE CASSEROLE

1 1/2 cups whole kernel corn,
*   fresh or frozen*
1/2 cup chopped onion
1/2 cup chopped green pepper
1/2 cup water
1 cup finely chopped yellow
*   summer squash or zucchini*
1 large (1 cup) tomato, chopped
1 cup (4 ounces) shredded
*   cheddar cheese, divided*

2/3 cup corn meal
1/2 cup milk
2 eggs, slightly beaten
3/4 teaspoon salt
1/4 teaspoon pepper
Several dashes hot pepper
*   sauce*
Tomato slices
Bell pepper slices

COMBINE corn, onion, green pepper, and water in
medium saucepan.

BRING to a boil, then REDUCE heat.

COVER and SIMMER 5 minutes. Do not drain.

COMBINE squash, tomato, 3/4 cup cheese, corn meal, milk,
eggs, salt, pepper, and hot pepper sauce.

ADD undrained vegetables.

MIX and TURN into greased 1 1/2-quart casserole.

MICROWAVE on high 10 minutes, turning casserole once,
OR
BAKE uncovered at 350° for 45 to 50 minutes or until
heated through.

TOP with remaining cheese and tomato and bell pepper slices.

Yield: 8 servings

Variation . . .

ITALIAN VEGETABLE CASSEROLE

ADD 1/2 teaspoon oregano or basil.
SUBSTITUTE 1 cup shredded mozzarella for cheddar cheese.

If you can eat rye, try this . . .

RYE KRISP PIZZA

SPREAD Rye Krisp in a flat pan. COVER with tomato paste.
ADD crumbled cooked hamburger or sliced sausage.
SPRINKLE with shredded mozzarella or jack cheese.
MICROWAVE 2 to 3 minutes, or BROIL until cheese melts.

If you have to stay away from all grains, this recipe is not for you!

ITALIAN RYE KRISP QUICHE

11 Rye Krisp crackers,
  crushed, reserving 1 tablespoon
3 tablespoons margarine, melted
1/4 cup chopped zucchini
1/2 cup (2 ounces) grated
  mozzarella cheese
3 eggs
1/4 cup plain yogurt

2 tablespoons chopped
  tomato
1/4 teaspoon Italian herb
  dressing
1/4 teaspoon salt
1 6-ounce can crab
  (optional)

PREHEAT oven to 350°.

GREASE 8-inch pie pan.

COMBINE crackers, margarine, and zucchini.

PRESS into bottom and sides of pan.

TOP with cheese.

BEAT eggs.

ADD yogurt, tomato, herb dressing, and salt.

POUR over cheese.

SPRINKLE reserved crumbs on top.

BAKE 30 minutes or until set.

LET STAND 5 minutes.

ZUCCHINI GARDEN STIR-FRY

1 cup green pepper strips
1 cup zucchini slices
1/2 cup onion rings
1/2 teaspoon oregano
1 tablespoon cooking oil

1/2 cup cherry tomato
  halves
3/4 cup (4 ounces) crumbled
  feta cheese

COMBINE green pepper, zucchini, onion, oregano, and oil in 1 1/2-quart microwavable bowl.

MICROWAVE on high 4 minutes, STIRRING after 2 minutes.

ADD tomatoes and MICROWAVE 1 minute.

TOP with cheese.

OR

SAUTE green peppers, zucchini, onion, oregano, and oil in large saucepan until tender but crisp, about 10 minutes.

ADD tomato and SAUTE 1 more minute.

ADD cheese.

Yield: 4 servings

*Angelica Germana and I have known each other for 55 years!
She made this for our St. Ambrose Grammar School reunion.*

ZUCCHINI ANGELICA

*4 eggs, slightly beaten
3 cups thinly sliced zucchini
1 cup Biscuit Mix (p. 14)
1/2 cup chopped onion
1/2 cup grated cheese
2 tablespoons chopped fresh
    parsley*

*1/2 teaspoon salt
1/2 teaspoon oregano
Pepper to taste
Fresh garlic to taste
1/2 cup oil*

PREHEAT oven to 350°.

GREASE oblong pan.

COMBINE all ingredients in greased pan.

BAKE at 350° for 30 to 40 minutes or until brown.

*Great for soups, stews, and cooked veggies.
Try a tablespoon in a pot of stew.*

HERB SEASONING MIX

*2 tablespoons dried dill weed
2 tablespoons dried parsley
1 tablespoon cumin seeds or 1 teaspoon ground cumin
1 tablespoon coriander seeds or 1 teaspoon ground coriander
1 tablespoon dried celery leaves or 1 teaspoon celery seeds*

*1 tablespoon caraway seeds
1 tablespoon fennel seeds*

PROCESS all ingredients in blender or processor.

STORE tightly capped in a cool, dark place for up to 6 months.

For your stale breadcrumbs . . .

SPINACH-STUFFED PEPPERS

2 large green, red, or yellow peppers
2 slices bacon, diced
1 cup sliced fresh mushrooms
1 small carrot, shredded
20 ounces canned or frozen spinach, drained
2 tablespoons wheat-free bread crumbs
1 tablespoon Herb Seasoning Mix (see recipe on previous page)

CUT peppers lengthwise and REMOVE seeds.

ARRANGE cut side down in microwavable dish.

COVER and MICROWAVE on high 2 to 3 minutes.

DRAIN and SET ASIDE.

PLACE bacon in 1-quart casserole; COVER with paper towels.

MICROWAVE on high 2 to 4 minutes, until crisp.

REMOVE bacon, but LEAVE drippings in casserole.

ADD mushrooms and carrot.

COVER and MICROWAVE on high 3 to 4 minutes.

DRAIN.

STIR in spinach and bread crumbs.

FILL pepper halves with spinach mixture.

MICROWAVE uncovered on high 3 to 5 minutes, until heated.

TOP with bacon.

Yield: 4 servings

GRANDMA'S BALTIMORE CRAB CAKES

(You will need additional time.)

1 teaspoon dry mustard
1/4 teaspoon EACH black and
* cayenne pepper, mixed*
1 small egg
1/3 cup (5 tablespoons)
* mayonnaise*

1 pound crab meat (back fin)
Parsley
1/2 cup wheat-free bread
* crumbs*
Oil for frying

COMBINE ingredients.

REFRIGERATE 1 day.

FORM into patties about 3/4 inch thick and 3 inches in diameter.

FRY in large skillet until brown on both sides.

Yield: 4 to 6 cakes

CRAB IMPERIAL

1 recipe Grandma's Baltimore Crab Cakes (see recipe above)
Mayonnaise
Paprika

PREHEAT oven to 350°.

GREASE ramekins (small oven-proof dishes).

PILE crab cake mixture into ramekins.

DOT with mayonnaise and SPRINKLE with paprika.

BAKE uncovered at 350° for 20 to 25 minutes.

FRIED CLAMS

24 clams
1 cup corn flour
2 eggs, beaten with a little water
2 cups wheat-free bread or cracker crumbs
Vegetable oil
Butter
Tartar sauce or hot mustard sauce

SHUCK and WASH clams well in colander under running water.
If clams have not had a corn meal bath (see below), OPEN stomachs
with sharp knife and SCRAPE out contents.
DRY between towels.
CUT away black neck skin.
DIP clams in flour, then egg-water mixture, and lastly crumbs.
SAUTE until golden in a combination of 3 parts vegetable oil to 2
parts butter.
SERVE with tartar sauce or hot mustard sauce.

Corn Meal Bath:
SOAK 1 quart clams and 1/4 cup corn meal in 1 gallon water 3 hours
or overnight.

*Brown rice has more fiber and other good things for you
than does white rice.*

PLAIN RICE

1 cup brown rice (see note)
2 1/2 cups water (see note)

PLACE ingredients in top of double boiler.
COOK covered, slowly until liquid is absorbed, about 30 to 35 minutes.

Note: For white rice, use 2 cups water and cook about 25 minutes.

Note: Substitute beef or chicken broth for 1 cup water.

ORANGE RAISIN RICE

1/4 cup oil
2 large onions, chopped
*1 cup cooked wild rice
  (see note)*
*3 cups cooked long grain
  rice (see note)*
1 cup dark raisins
1/2 cup chopped almonds

1/2 cup chopped parsley
1/4 cup grated orange peel
*1 teaspoon freshly ground
  pepper*
Orange slices
Parsley sprigs

HEAT onions in oil in large saucepan.
ADD cooked rice and MIX well.
STIR in raisins, chopped parsley, orange peel, and pepper.
GARNISH with orange slices and parsley.

Note: You may substititute rice types, but keep the total quantity
at 4 cups.

Yield: 12 servings

This is my favorite potluck contribution.
Be prepared for recipe requests!

CURRIED RICE SALAD

(You will need additional time.)

1/4 cup Italian salad dressing
2 cups cooked rice
1 10-ounce package frozen peas,
  cooked
1 cup diced celery
1/2 cup chopped onions
1 7-ounce can tiny shrimp
  (optional)

Water chestnuts or 1/2 cup
  nuts (optional)
3/4 cup mayonnaise
1/2 teaspoon curry powder
1/4 teaspoon salt
Olive slices
Green pepper slices

COMBINE rice and salad dressing.

LET STAND for 1 hour or more.

ADD peas, celery, and onions.

ADD shrimp and water chestnuts or nuts, if using.

COMBINE in another bowl mayonnaise, curry powder, and salt.

COMBINE mixtures.

GARNISH with olives and green pepper.

RICE COMBINATIONS

To avoid hidden wheat or dairy contents, use homemade soups. Otherwise, use 1 14-ounce can of soup for each combination.

1. Cream of mushroom soup
*   or white sauce*
2 cups peas
1 7-ounce can small
*   shrimp, crabmeat, or salmon*
2 cups cooked rice

4. Cream of mushroom soup
*   or white sauce*
2 cups green beans
1 7-ounce can small shrimp
2 cups cooked rice

2. Tomato soup
1 tablespoon cornstarch
2 cups succotash
1 pound meatballs
2 cups cooked rice

5. Tomato soup
1 tablespoon cornstarch
2 cups pea
1 can tuna
2 cups cooked rice

3. Tomato soup
1 tablespoon cornstarch
2 cups mixed vegetables
Sliced sausage
2 cups cooked rice

COMBINE one recipe in a skillet and COOK on medium heat until thoroughly heated, about 20 minutes.

*It won't be the same, but you can substitute tofu for cheese,
if you must stay away from dairy foods.*

BLUE CHEESE PASTA

4 cups water
2 cups wheat-free noodles (p. 44) with
  1 cup noodle cooking water reserved
3 cups frozen broccoli, carrots, and cauliflower
2 tablespoons rice or bean flour
2 tablespoons butter or margarine
Salt and pepper to taste
1/2 cup (2 ounces) blue cheese
1/3 cup sour cream, yogurt, or sour cream substitute
1 or 2 cans clams, drained (optional)

BOIL water in stock pot.

ADD pasta.

BOIL 8 to 10 minutes or until almost tender.

ADD frozen vegetables and COOK 5 to 7 minutes more.

DRAIN, reserving 1 cup liquid in separate container.

MIX flour and butter or margarine with salt and pepper in pot.

ADD reserved liquid and STIR until bubbly.

ADD pasta and vegetable mixture.

REMOVE from heat.

ADD blue cheese and sour cream, yogurt, or sour crean substitute.

ADD clams, if using.

RETURN to heat and HEAT through.

TOP with additional cheese.

SERVE at once.

In spite of my intent to keep recipes simple, husband Ed says that I had better include this one anyway. It's more involved, but it is excellent and was originally made without wheat.

BLINTZES

6 eggs
1 teaspoon salt
1 cup potato starch
2 cups water
Oil for frying

Filling:

1 pound farmer's or ricotta cheese
1 pound pot cheese or well-drained cottage cheese (see note)
1 tablespoon melted butter
1 teaspoon granulated sugar
2 eggs
1/2 teaspoon salt

BLEND eggs and salt in blender or processor.

ADD potato starch and water.

BLEND until smooth, then POUR into pitcher.

HEAT 6-inch skillet until very hot.

OIL well.

POUR in 3 tablespoons batter and SWIRL to cover pan.

POUR off excess.

COOK on only one side until firm, about 1 minute.

TURN onto counter or board to COOL.

COVER each blintz with wax paper when cool and STACK.

REPEAT until all batter is used.

COVER stack with towel.

STIR all filling ingredients together until well blended.

SPREAD blintzes on counter.

SPOON heaping tablespoon of filling into center of each blintz.

ROLL up, tucking in sides.

COVER and REFRIGERATE for 2 hours minimum or 2 days maximum. If stacking, LAYER with wax paper.

SAUTE in butter over low heat until golden brown on both sides.

SERVE with sour cream, fresh fruit, or both.

Note: You may substitute tofu for cheese or use a fruit filling.

POTATO LATKES (PANCAKES)

6 medium potatoes	*1/2 cup bean flour*
1 onion	*1 teaspoon salt*
2 eggs	*Oil for frying*

PEEL and GRATE potatoes into mixing bowl.

SQUEEZE out liquid.

PEEL and GRATE onion into potatoes.

ADD eggs, flour, and salt and STIR.

HEAT oil in heavy frying pan, using enough oil to cover pancakes.

DROP batter from a spoon into hot oil, making pancakes 2 to 3 inches in diameter.

FRY over moderate heat until brown on one side, then TURN and brown other side.

LIFT out and DRAIN on paper towel.

Yield: 4 to 6 servings

NON-DAIRY SCALLOPED POTATOES

SLICE potatoes thinly with a processor.

PLACE in saucepan.

COVER barely with water and HEAT until boiling.

COOK covered at medium heat until potatoes are soft and have made their own sauce.

SEASON according to taste.

A very filling non-wheat meal . . .

SWISS POTATO PIE

2 pounds red or new potatoes
3 tablespoons butter, divided
2 pounds (2 bunches) Swiss
  chard, coarsely chopped
1 shallot, minced

2 cloves garlic, minced
3 tablespoons balsamic vinegar
Dash pepper
Pepper to taste
2 cups chicken stock

PREHEAT oven to 375°.

BUTTER large, shallow casserole dish.

SLICE potatoes thinly and SET ASIDE.

MELT 2 tablespoons butter in large skillet.

ADD Swiss chard, shallot, and garlic.

COOK Swiss chard until wilted, then ADD vinegar, nutmeg, and pepper.

ALTERNATE layers of potatoes and Swiss chard in casserole dish.

POUR chicken stock over layers so they are just covered.

DOT with remaining 1 tablespoon butter.

BAKE uncovered at 375° for 50 to 60 minutes

OR

MICROWAVE at 50 percent power for 20 minutes.

LET stand 10 minutes and SERVE.

Yield: 8 servings

Here's another way to use Biscuit Mix.

RING AROUND THE VEGGIES

3 cups Biscuit Mix (pg. 14)
2/3 to 1 cup water or milk
1 pound (3 or 4 small)
  red potatoes
1 1/2 cups cooked broccoli
2 tablespoons canola oil
  or butter
2 tablespoons bean or
  rice flour

1/2 teaspoon salt
2 cups rice or soy milk
1/3 cup shredded cheese
  (see note)
1 tablespoon dried parsley
1 tablespoon basil (optional)

PREHEAT oven to 350°.

MIX biscuit mix with water or milk.

DROP by spoonfuls around edge of 9-inch pie pan, leaving center
open. BAKE at 350° for 25 minutes.

CUT potatoes in half and COOK in water over medium heat
until tender.

COOK broccoli in small amount of water about 8 minutes.
DRAIN.

MIX oil, flour, and salt in saucepan or skillet to make a paste.

HEAT and ADD rice or milk and cheese.

STIR until thickened.

ADD drained potatoes and broccoli to sauce.

SPOON potato-sauce mixture into biscuit ring and SERVE.

Note: If dairy is a problem, try almond or soy cheese from your health
food store.

Options: Experiment with different kinds of vegetables and sauces. A
little ham and 2 tablespoons sherry is also good!

As close as we can come to a real . . .

PIZZA CRUST

1 1/2 cups rice flour	*1/2 teaspoon salt*
1 1/2 cups bean flour	*1/2 cup milk or water*
3 teaspoons xanthan gum	*1/2 cup oil*
3 teaspoons baking powder	

PREHEAT oven to 350°.

COMBINE flours, xanthan gum, baking powder, and salt in large bowl.

ADD milk or water and oil and MIX well.

KNEAD until smooth, about 10 minutes.

ROLL onto oiled pizza pan or cookie sheet.

BRUSH cooking oil lightly with fingers around edges.

To Make a Great Pizza:

PREPARE pizza crust (see recipe above).

SPREAD with 1 can tomato sauce.

ADD oregano, basil, or both to taste.

COVER with grated mozzarella or jack cheese. (see note)

ADD whatever suits your fancy: crumbled hamburger, sliced sausage, olives, onions, tomatoes, anchovies, mushrooms, pineapple, cooked shrimp.

SPRINKLE lightly with grated Parmesan cheese. (see note)

BAKE at 350° for 10 minutes, then at 400° for 10 minutes.

SERVE hot, or freeze and reheat.

Note: If dairy is a problem, you may want to try one of the "fake" cheeses made from tofu or almond, found at your health food store.

This is very filling, and you can vary the meat portion.

HEARTY STUFFED POTATOES

2 large baking potatoes
1/2 pound pork sausage
1 medium onion, chopped
1 medium green pepper,
   sliced
1 8-ounce can tomato
   sauce

1/2 cup water
1/2 teaspoon dried
   oregano leaves
Dash hot pepper sauce

PREHEAT oven to 375°.

SCRUB each potato and PRICK with a fork.

BAKE at 375° for 40 to 60 minutes or MICROWAVE on high for
8 to 10 minutes, rotating after 4 minutes.

COOK pork sausage, onion, and green pepper in large frying pan
over medium high heat 5 to 6 minutes.

POUR off drippings.

STIR in tomato sauce, water, oregano, and hot pepper sauce.

COOK over low heat 7 to 10 minutes, stirring occasionally.

CUT potatoes in half lengthwise and gently PUSH ends to open.

SPOON sausage mixture into each potato half and SERVE.

Yield: 4 servings

*My grown children would rate their mom a "zero" if she
didn't fix this dish for the holidays!*

HOLIDAY SWEET POTATOES

*3 large sweet potatoes
or yams
1/2 cup frozen orange juice
concentrate, thawed
2 tablespoons brown sugar
1/2 cup walnut or pecan
halves*

*1/4 cup butter or 1/8 cup oil
6 slices cooked bacon,
chopped
2 cups miniature marshmallows*

PREHEAT oven to 350°.

CUT sweet potatoes or yams into 1/2-inch chunks.

ADD water just to cover and BOIL until easily pierced with fork.

PLACE in 2-quart casserole dish.

COMBINE orange juice, brown sugar, walnuts or pecans, butter or
oil, and bacon and POUR over potatoes.

TOP with marshmallows.

BAKE at 350° for 20 minutes or until marshmallows are light brown.

If you don't have noodles, you can still make lasagne . . .

POTATO LASAGNE

1/4 cup oil
1/2 cup rice flour
2 cups rice milk
2 cups chicken broth
1/4 teaspoon nutmeg
1 cup (4 ounces) EACH
  shredded Havarti,
  provolone, and Swiss
  cheese or
  3 cups of all one kind

Pepper
5 large (about 2 1/2 pounds)
  russet potatoes
1 large red onion,
  thinly sliced
1/4 pound prosciutto or ham,
  slivered
10 ounces frozen chopped
  spinach, thawed
Parmesan cheese

HEAT oil and flour in 2-quart saucepan until bubbly.

REMOVE from heat and ADD milk, chicken broth, and nutmeg.

HEAT until boiling.

REMOVE from heat and ADD 1 cup grated cheese at a time.

STIR until smooth and ADD pepper to taste.

PREHEAT oven to 375°. BUTTER 9 x 13-inch baking dish.

PEEL and slice potatoes. ARRANGE 1/3 slices in bottom of pan.

COVER with 1/2 onion, 1/2 of prosciutto or ham, and 1/2 drained spinach. POUR 1/3 cheese sauce over top.

REPEAT layers, ending with potatoes and cheese sauce.

BAKE covered at 375° for 30 minutes.

REMOVE cover and CONTINUE baking 1 hour.

SPRINKLE Parmesan cheese over lasagne and BAKE 5 minutes.

LET stand 10 minutes before serving.

Yield: 6 servings

COUNTRY CABBAGE

1/2 pound lean ground pork
1/2 pound lean ground beef
1 large cabbage, coarsely
  chopped
1 medium red onion,
  chopped
1/2 green pepper, chopped

1 sprig parsley or
  1 tablespoon dried parsley
1/2 teaspoon salt
1/8 teaspoon black pepper
1 quart canned tomatoes
1 cup tomato puree
2 or 3 fresh basil leaves
  or 1 tablespoon dried basil

BROWN ground meat and POUR off grease, leaving 2 tablespoons.

PLACE all ingredients in large stew pot.

COVER and SIMMER until meat and vegetables are tender, about
45 minutes.

SERVE in soup bowls with sourdough bread (p. 80).

RED CABBAGE

1 medium-size head red cabbage
4 tablespoons butter or margarine
2 tart apples, chopped
6 whole cloves
1 glass (4 to 5 ounces) red wine (optional)

SLICE cabbage thinly and CHOP.

COMBINE cabbage, butter, apples, and cloves.

COOK about 15 minutes until tender. REMOVE cloves.

ADD wine, if using, and SIMMER 1 minute more.

CHEESE-STUFFED SQUASH

2 or 3 large zucchini or
　crookneck squash
1 small onion, minced
2 tablespoons bacon drippings
　or butter or oil
1/2 teaspoon salt
1/4 teaspoon pepper
1 cup fine wheat-free
　bread crumbs

1/2 cup sliced, cooked
　mushrooms
1/3 cup shredded cheddar
　cheese (see note)
3 slices bacon,
　partially cooked

CUT the squash in half lengthwise.

MICROWAVE until barely tender, about 5 minutes per pound.

COOL and CUT in half crosswise.

PREHEAT oven to 400°.

SCOOP out pulp, leaving shells about 1/4 inch thick.

COOK onion in skillet in bacon drippings, butter, or oil until tender but not browned.

ADD squash pulp, salt, pepper, bread crumbs, and mushrooms.

MIX well and SPOON into squash shells.

ARRANGE in shallow 2-quart baking dish and TOP with cheese.

CUT bacon strips in halves and ARRANGE on top of squash.

BAKE at 400° for 15 minutes or until browned.

Yield: 6 servings

Note: If you cannot tolerate dairy cheese, try some almond or soy cheese from your health food store.

This is a very adaptable dish.
You can experiment with many vegetables.

STIR-FRIED RICE

1/2 onion, chopped
2 stalks celery, chopped
2 to 3 cups cold cooked rice
1 egg, beaten
2 tablespoons tamari

SAUTE onion and celery in skillet.

ADD rice.

ADD egg and tamari and STIR well.

HEAT thoroughly and SERVE.

Note: Salmon tastes delicious added to the stir-fry, but you may add any leftover vegetables, meat, or both.

FILBERT RICE

4 cups cooked basmati or
  brown rice
1/2 cup coarsely
  ground filberts
1/4 cup dried parsley

3 tablespoons canola oil
Salt to taste
1/3 cup grated
  Parmesan cheese

PREHEAT oven to 300°.

COMBINE rice, filberts, parsley, oil, and salt in ovenproof casserole.

PLACE in oven and WARM at 300° for 5 to 10 minutes.

SPRINKLE cheese on top.

BROIL 3 to 5 minutes.

There are several ways to do . . .

FRIED GREEN TOMATOES

6 large green tomatoes,
    ends trimmed, sliced thick
1 egg, beaten
Corn meal, corn flour,
    rice flour, or arrowroot

Bacon grease or
    cooking oil

PLACE beaten egg in shallow bowl.

DIP tomato slices into egg.

COAT with corn meal or flour, on a plate.

FRY one side in skillet in 1/4 inch grease or oil.

TURN and FRY other side.

LIFT onto platter and SERVE.

Another Old-Fashioned Way:

This tastes very good, although it contains quite a bit more fat.

POUR 3/4 cup heavy cream or non-dairy creamer into skillet after removing tomatoes.

ADD 1 tablespoon basil or parsley.

COOK slowly, STIRRING to scrape up browned bits. Do not boil.

POUR over tomatoes and SERVE at once.

Yield: 6 servings

Don't throw out those green tomatoes at the end of summer.
Slice them, coat them, and freeze them.

FRIED GREEN TOMATOES
FOR ANOTHER DAY!

SLICE tomatoes 3/4 inch thick.

COAT in corn meal or non-wheat flour of your choosing.

SEASON with salt, pepper, and basil.

FREEZE on a cookie sheet in one layer.

When frozen, TRANSFER to containers.

PAN FRY without thawing for 10 minutes, TURNING once.

You can do so many good things with your "not-so-successful bread"
experiments. Save your leftovers for recipes like the following . . .

STEWED BREAD

1/2 onion, sliced
1/2 cup chopped green pepper or celery
1 29-ounce can tomatoes
1 teaspoon basil
2 to 3 slices not-so-successful bread, cubed

SAUTE onion and pepper or celery in large skillet until softened.

ADD tomatoes and basil.

ADD bread cubes to mixture.

HEAT thoroughly.

The aroma when this is baking is out of this world!
Husband Ed tells me that kugel is usually served as a side
dish with dinner, but it can also be a dessert.

APPLE KUGEL

1/2 pound (about 4 cups loose)
Noodles (wheat-free),
uncooked (p. 44)
1/2 cup + 2 tablespoons
unsulfured molasses
1/4 cup boiling water
4 large eggs, beaten
3 tablespoons oat bran (optional)

1/2 teaspoon salt
1 teaspoon vanilla
2 teaspoons dried basil
2 large apples, peeled, cored,
and chopped
1 cup raisins
1 teaspoon cinnamon

COOK noodles and DRAIN well.

COOK molasses in large skillet on low heat until mixture bubbles.

ADD boiling water, REMOVE from heat, and ADD noodles.

ADD eggs to the skillet with bran, if using, and salt, vanilla,
and basil.

GREASE a 2-quart casserole.

POUR in mixture and gently ADD apples and raisins.

SPRINKLE cinnamon on top.

BAKE at 350° for about 30 minutes or until top is crisp.

Yield: 6 to 8 servings

ANTIPASTO

1 clove garlic
1 cup green pepper, in 1-inch pieces
1 cup sliced mushrooms
1/2 cup diced jack or Swiss cheese
1 6 1/2-ounce jar artichoke hearts
3 or 4 anchovies, cut in small pieces
1 tablespoon dried or 1/4 cup chopped fresh parsley
1 tablespoon dried or 1/4 cup chopped fresh basil
3 tablespoons wine or cider vinegar
Lettuce leaves
1/4 cup olive oil
Salt and pepper to taste
1 tablespoon Dijon-style mustard (optional + see note)

RUB a bowl with garlic.

COMBINE all ingredients in bowl.

SERVE on lettuce leaves.

Note: Check the vinegar used in the mustard if you must avoid grains. People with gluten problems need to avoid distilled vinegars. Apple cider and wine vinegars are OK!

A wonderful old favorite and so good for you . . .

TURKEY SALAD

4 cups chopped turkey
1 cup chopped apple
1 cup chopped walnuts
1 cup grapes

1 cup pineapple tidbits
1/2 cup mayonnaise
  or yogurt
Lettuce leaves

COMBINE all ingredients and SERVE on lettuce.

A filling, easy-to-fix dish.

CHICKEN AVOCADO

2 avocados, split, with
  pits removed
Few drops lemon juice
1 7-ounce can chicken
1/4 cup finely
  chopped tomato

Spicy-sweet French
  dressing
Bacon bits

SCOOP out avocado pulp, CUT into chunks, and RESERVE shells.

SPRINKLE chunks with lemon juice.

DRAIN chicken and BREAK apart.

MIX gently chicken, avocado, and tomato.

SPOON into avocado shells.

TOP with salad dressing and bacon bits.

Soups

CLIMB THE MOUNTAINS AND GET THEIR GOOD TIDINGS;
NATURE'S PEACE WILL FLOW INTO YOU AS SUNSHINE INTO FLOWERS;
THE WINDS WILL BLOW THEIR FRESHNESS INTO YOU AND THE STORMS THEIR ENERGY, AND CARES WILL DROP OFF LIKE AUTUMN LEAVES.

—John Muir

CHICKEN STOCK

Carcass of roast turkey or chicken, with
broken up bones
2 large onions, chopped (use processor)
3 carrots, peeled and chopped
1 to 2 leeks, white and green parts, thinly sliced
3 whole garlic cloves
Handful fresh parsley
2 bay leaves
1 teaspoon dried thyme
Several black peppercorns
12 cups cold water

BRING all ingredients to a boil in a large covered stock pot.

LOWER heat to a gentle simmer for 3 hours, partly covered.

SKIM froth.

STRAIN through sieve, PRESSING out solids.

LET COOL and REFRIGERATE or FREEZE.

Here's a milk-free cream of potato soup.

POTATO SOUP

4 cups chicken or turkey stock
2 cups diced potatoes
1 carrot, grated
2 cups chopped onions,
  sauteed (optional)
1 tablespoon Herb Seasoning
  Mix (p. 114)

1 teaspoon dried dill weed
6 drops hot pepper sauce
1/4 cup parsley leaves
1/4 teaspoon caraway seeds
  (optional + see note)

COMBINE stock, potatoes, onions if using, herb mix, dill weed, and pepper sauce in a stockpot.

BRING to a boil, then REDUCE heat.

SIMMER 25 to 30 minutes, until vegetables are soft.

TRANSFER 1 cup vegetables and broth to blender or processor.

PROCESS until smooth.

RETURN to pot and ADD parsley and caraway seeds, if using.

Note: Caraway seeds give a different flavor.

GARDEN POTATO SOUP

4 medium potatoes, peeled and diced
4 medium tomatoes, quartered
Few sprigs marjoram, thyme, or
 parsley, or 1/2 teaspoon
 your choice dried herbs

6 cups water
1 teaspoon salt
1 tablespoon butte

BOIL potatoes, tomatoes, herbs, and water in stockpot until soup
reaches a smooth consistency.

ADD salt and butter and SERVE.

Optional: PUREE cooked soup in blender or processor.

CREAMED VEGETABLE SOUP

Chopped veggies	*2 cups*	*3 cups*
Water or stock	*2 1/2 cups*	*6 1/4 cups*
Cornstarch or flour	*3 tablespoons*	*4 tablespoons*
Milk (see note)	*1 cup*	*1 1/2 cups*
Butter	*1 tablespoon*	*1 tablespoon*
Spices (see note)	*to taste*	*to taste*

COOK vegetables in water until tender, then CHOP.

PUREE vegetables.

DISSOLVE cornstarch or flour in milk.

ADD to puree.

BRING to boil.

ADD butter.

SEASON to taste with salt and pepper.

Note: You may add onion powder, basil, coriander, or whatever, to taste.

Note: You may use soy milk, coconut milk, or non-dairy creamer.

Yield: 4 or 6 cups

TOMATO SOUP

2 tablespoons butter
  or margarine
1 medium onion, chopped
1 large carrot, chopped
4 cups regular-strength
  chicken broth
1 15-ounce can
  tomato puree

3 tablespoons dried basil
3/4 teaspoon granulated
  sugar (optional)
1/2 teaspoon white pepper
Cheese croutons

MELT butter or margarine in 4-quart pot.

ADD onion and carrot and COOK until both are tender, 30 minutes.

STIR broth, tomato puree, basil, sugar, if using, and pepper.

BRING to boil and SIMMER covered about 15 minutes.

SCOOP vegetables into food processor or blender. PUREE.

POUR vegetable mixture back into pan.

HEAT.

LADLE into bowls. TOP with croutons.

Yield: 4 servings

A wonderful Spanish soup and so easy to make.
From the kitchen of Jim Knull, Grapeview, Wash.

GAZPACHO

1 cucumber, chopped
1/2 green pepper, chopped
1 small onion, finely chopped
2 tomatoes, chopped
4 cups tomato juice
3 tablespoons salad oil

2 tablespoons wine vinegar
1 tablespoon dried oregano
  or basil
1/2 avocado, diced
Salt and pepper to taste

MIX chopped vegetables and RESERVE about 1/2 cup mixture.

PLACE remaining ingredients in blender or processor and PUREE.

ADD reserved vegetables into soup.

COVER and CHILL at least 2 hours.

A wonderful way to start to your meal . . .

CIDER SOUP

2 quarts apple cider
1/2 cup granulated sugar
3 eggs, beaten
2 cups rice or soy milk
3 tablespoons rice or bean flour

Allspice or nutmeg to taste
3 cups wheat-free
   bread cubes (see note)
Butter or margarine

BOIL cider in large stockpot and SKIM if necessary.

COMBINE sugar, eggs, and milk.

ADD flour and allspice or nutmeg.

ADD milk mixture to cider.

BROWN bread cubes in butter or margarine.

SPRINKLE bread cubes on top and SERVE.

Note: Use some of your not-so-successful bread experiments.

Yield: 6 servings

BOUILLABAISSE

1/2 cup olive oil
1 carrot, chopped
2 onions, chopped
2 leeks, white and
  green parts, diced
1 clove garlic, pressed
Few grains saffron
1 lobster, cut in
  small pieces
1/2 pound shrimp, shelled
  and cleaned or 1/2 pound
  crab meat

3 pounds boned fish (any
  variety is good)
2 large tomatoes or 1 cup
  canned tomatoes, cut up
1 bay leaf
2 quarts boiling water
  or fish broth
1 dozen live mussels, clams,
  or oysters in shell
Salt and pepper
Juice of 1 lemon
1 cup white wine

PUT oil, carrots, onions, leeks, and garlic in a big kettle.

COOK until brown.

PREPARE lobster and shrimp and SET ASIDE.

ADD to kettle boned fish, tomatoes, bay leaf, saffron, and water
or broth.

SIMMER 20 minutes.

ADD all shellfish.

SIMMER until shells open, 5 minutes.

REMOVE top shells from mussels, clams, or oysters.

ADD salt and pepper to taste.

ADD lemon juice.

ADD 1 cup white wine.

BRING to simmer and SERVE.

Yield: 4 to 6 servings

Here is a painless way to increase your calcium.

KALE SOUP

1/2 cup chopped onions,
  sauteed
1 cup diced potatoes
2 cups minced kale

1 teaspoon salt
4 cups boiling water
  (see note)
3 tablespoons oil

COMBINE onions, potatoes, kale, oil, salt, and water in stockpot.

PUREE at least 3/4 of soup in processor or blender.

RETURN to pot and COOK 20 to 30 minutes.

Yield: 6 servings

Note: You may substitute 1 or 2 cups soy or rice milk.

MOBY DICK CHOWDER

2 cups kale or spinach, cooked
2 small cans clams or shrimp
2 cups rice or soy milk

1 tablespoon butter or
  canola oil
Salt and pepper
Dash nutmeg

DRAIN kale or spinach.

PUT in blender or processor with clams or shrimp, including juice.

PROCESS 10 seconds.

POUR into saucepan. ADD milk and BRING barely to a boil.

ADD butter or oil and seasonings.

Yield: 4 to 6 servings

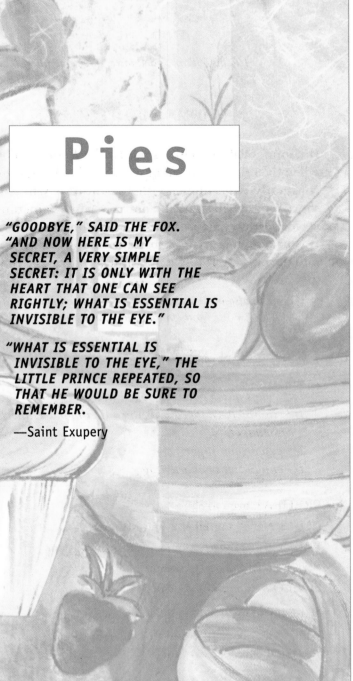

Pies

"GOODBYE," SAID THE FOX. "AND NOW HERE IS MY SECRET, A VERY SIMPLE SECRET: IT IS ONLY WITH THE HEART THAT ONE CAN SEE RIGHTLY; WHAT IS ESSENTIAL IS INVISIBLE TO THE EYE."

"WHAT IS ESSENTIAL IS INVISIBLE TO THE EYE," THE LITTLE PRINCE REPEATED, SO THAT HE WOULD BE SURE TO REMEMBER.

—Saint Exupery

Luckily, it's the good tastes one remembers best!

A WORD ABOUT PIE CRUST

If commercial pie makers adjust the flour-to-shortening ratio when the protein content of wheat varies, I suspect that we must constantly experiment with the ratio of wheat-free flour to shortening when we make our pie crusts. Sometimes the dough is wonderfully easy to roll out; other times it wants to tear apart. If your dough is giving you a difficult time, just press the dough into the pie pan. It is just not quite as pretty as a rolled-out crust.

You can also make a single pie crust by mixing a cereal grain and nut combination. An example:

CEREAL NUT PIE CRUST

1 1/2 cups quick oats, uncooked (see note)
1/2 cup finely chopped nuts, such as almonds, filberts, pecans, cashews, etc.
1/3 cup brown sugar
1/3 cup butter or shortening

PREHEAT oven to 350°.

COMBINE all ingredients and MIX well.

PRESS firmly onto bottom and sides of pie pan.

BAKE at 350° about 18 minutes.

FOLLOW the rest of your recipe.

Note: If you must avoid gluten, use rice cereals.

Write down your successes. It's all right to write in this book! Leave yourself a note for next time.

It's so nice to have rolls of pie crust in your freezer.
A delicious pie is then not such an overwhelming task.

PIE CRUST MIX

8 1/2 cups bean flour	*2 tablespoons salt*
8 1/2 cups white rice flour	*1 3-pound can shortening*
6 tablespoons xanthan gum	*2 1/2 cups cold water*

COMBINE flours, xanthan gum, and salt.

MIX with a pastry blender.

CUT in shortening and MIX until particles are the size of peas.

ADD cold water and MIX gently just enough to dampen entire mix.

If mixture is too sticky, SPRINKLE a little flour over it.

DIVIDE dough and SHAPE into 10 oblong rolls.

WRAP rolls separately in plastic wrap.

FREEZE.

Yield: 10 double pie crusts

Note: Xanthan gum is vital to the manageability of the dough.

DOUBLE PIE CRUST

THAW dough in refrigerator overnight OR BARELY THAW it
in a microwave oven.

DIVIDE roll into 2 pieces.

ROLL out one piece on lightly floured pastry cloth about
1/8 inch thick.

WRAP dough around rolling pin and TRANSFER to pie pan.

ADD filling and COVER with remaining rolled-out piece.

CRIMP or FLUTE edges.

BAKE according to pie directions.

SINGLE PIE CRUST

THAW dough in refrigerator overnight OR BARELY THAW it
in a microwave oven.

PREHEAT oven to 400°.

ROLL 1/2 of pastry to desired thickness.

TRANSFER to pie pan.

BAKE 15 minutes or until lightly browned.

COOL before filling.

If you haven't any pastry dough and you need a pie now,
here's a recipe for one double crust.

DOUBLE PIE CRUST 2

1 cup rice flour
1 cup bean flour
2 teaspoons xanthan gum

1/2 teaspoon salt
3/4 cup vegetable shortening
1/3 cup cold water

MIX flours, xanthan gum, and salt with a pastry blender.

CUT in shortening and MIX until particles are pea-sized.

ADD water and MIX gently just enough to dampen entire mixture.
If mixture is too sticky, SPRINKLE a little flour over it.

DIVIDE dough into 2 rolls.

ROLL each piece on lightly floured pastry cloth to desired thickness
to fit pan size.

WRAP dough around rolling pin and TRANSFER to pie pan.

ADD filling and COVER with remaining rolled out piece.

CRIMP or FLUTE edges.

This cookielike crust is best on a slightly tart pie.

SWEET DOUGH

1/2 cup rice flour
1/2 cup bean flour
Pinch of salt
1 cup brown sugar
1 teaspoon xanthan gum

1/2 cup shortening
1/2 teaspoon baking soda
1/4 cup buttermilk
   or applesauce
1/2 cup shortening

COMBINE flours, salt, brown sugar, and xanthan gum.

ADD shortening and BLEND until crumbly.

DISSOLVE baking soda in buttermilk or applesauce and ADD to flour mixture.

ADD more buttermilk or applesauce if dough is too stiff.

ROLL on floured board and CUT into strips.

PLACE on top of pies.

If you have dough left, cut it into doughnut shapes, twisting into figure 8s before baking briefly in a medium oven.

To keep the bottom crust from getting soggy brush it with egg white before filling. Brushing the top crust makes it look and taste great. These fruit pies even freeze well.

APPLE PIE

6 to 8 (6 cups) tart apples (see note)
1/2 cup honey (1/4 to 1 cup sugar)
3 tablespoons cornstarch (1 tablespoon with older apples)
1 teaspoon cinnamon
Dash salt
1 9-inch Double Pie Crust, unbaked (p. 152)

PREHEAT oven to 350°.

MIX apples, honey or sugar, cornstarch, cinnamon, and salt in a microwaveable bowl.

MICROWAVE on high 4 minutes, STIRRING after 2 minutes (see note).

POUR mixture into pastry-lined pie pan and DOT with butter.

COVER with second crust, CRIMP edges, and CUT 3 or 4 steam vents in top.

BAKE at 350° for 40 minutes. If you skip the microwave step, increase baking time to 1 hour.

Note: If apples are not tart, add 1 tablespoon lemon juice or grated lemon peel. For older apples, use more seasoning.

Note: Square dancer Marjorie Jacobs taught me that microwaving the filling cuts down on baking time.

MARIONBERRY (OR BOYSENBERRY) PIE

4 cups fresh berries (see note)
3 to 4 tablespoons cornstarch
3/4 cup honey or
   1 cup granulated sugar

1 tablespoon butter or
   margarine
1 10-inch Double Pie Crust,
   unbaked (p. 152)

PREHEAT oven to 375°.

MIX berries with cornstarch in a microwaveable bowl.

POUR honey or sugar over berries.

MICROWAVE on high 3 to 5 minutes.

POUR mixture into pastry-lined pie pan and DOT with butter.

COVER with second crust, CRIMP edges, and CUT 3 or 4 steam vents in top.

BAKE at 375° for 30 minutes or until brown. If you skip the microwave step, increase baking time to 1 hour.

Note: Marionberries or boysenberries work great in this recipe.

PEACH PIE

1 cup brown sugar
4 tablespoons cornstarch or wheat-free flour
Dash salt
6 cups fresh sliced peaches
1/4 teaspoon almond extract
1 tablespoon butter or margarine
1 10-inch Double Pie Crust, unbaked (p. 152)

PREHEAT oven to 350°.

MIX sugar, cornstarch or flour, and salt in a large microwaveable bowl.

STIR in fruit and almond extract.

MICROWAVE on high 3 to 5 minutes.

POUR mixture into pastry-lined pie pan and DOT with butter.

COVER with second crust, CRIMP edges, and CUT 3 or 4 steam vents in top.

BAKE at 350° for 40 minutes. If you skip the microwave step, increase baking time to 1 hour.

*Grandma Potts, very much a city lady, picked blueberries
with us in the country . . . and I remember two little boys
who stole a whole pie and ate it under the trees!*

BLUEBERRY PIE

*5 cups fresh or frozen blueberries
3 tablespoons rice flour
1 cup graulated sugar or 3/4 cup honey
1/4 teaspoon salt
1 tablespoon lemon juice (omit if using wild berries)
1 tablespoon butter or margarine
1 10-inch Double Pie Crust, unbaked (p. 152)*

PREHEAT oven to 350°.

MIX berries, flour, sugar or honey, salt, and lemon juice gently in a
microwaveable bowl.

MICROWAVE on high 3 minutes.

POUR mixture into pastry-lined pie pan and DOT with butter.

COVER with second crust, CRIMP edges, and CUT 3 or 4 steam
vents in top.

BAKE at 350° for 40 minutes. If you skip the microwave step,
increase baking time to 1 hour.

*Out here in Oregon, the strawberry fields open about the
first week in June. Pick enough for pie!*

STRAWBERRY PIE

1 9-inch Single Pie Crust,
  baked (p. 152)
1 to 2 cups ripe whole
  strawberries
2 cups crushed strawberries,
  divided

1 cup granulated sugar
3 tablespoons cornstarch
1/2 teaspoon lemon juice
Grated lemon or orange peel
1 tablespoon butter
Non-dairy whipped topping

FILL baked pie crust with whole berries.

BRING to a boil and SIMMER 1 1/2 cups crushed berries and sugar.

MIX cornstarch into remaining 1/2 cup crushed strawberries.

ADD to cooked mixture. ADD lemon juice and rind.

COOK until clear. ADD 1 tablespoon butter to give a glazed look.

POUR over whole berries and CHILL.

TOP with non-dairy whipped topping, before serving.

BING CHERRY (SWEET CHERRY) PIE

1 10-inch Double Pie Crust
  unbaked (p. 152)
5 to 6 cups fresh cherries, pitted
2 to 3 tablespoons tapioca

1/2 cup brown sugar,
1 teaspoon lemon
Butter

PREHEAT oven to 350°. FILL pastry-lined pie pan with cherries.

ADD tapioca, lemon, and brown sugar. DOT with butter.

COVER with second crust, CRIMP edges, and CUT 3 or 4 steam
vents in top.

BAKE at 350° for 40 minutes or until crust is nicely browned.

This is for Little Jack Horner . . .

PLUM PIE

1 9-inch Double Pie Crust,
  unbaked (p. 152)
2 tablespoons corn meal
3 cups Greengage plums, halved and pitted

1 teaspoon cinnamon
1 cup granulated sugar
2 teaspoons powdered sugar

PREHEAT oven to 325°. LINE pie pan with pastry.

SPRINKLE corn meal over crust. ADD plums.

SPRINKLE cinnamon and sugar over plums.

COVER with second crust, CRIMP edges, and CUT 3 or 4 steam

vents in top. BAKE at 325° about 45 minutes.

REMOVE from oven. SPRINKLE powdered sugar on crust.

AMISH PIE

1 9-inch Single Pie Crust,
  baked (p. 152)
1 cup dark brown sugar
1/4 cup boiling water
Walnut-size knob of butter
  or margarine
3 cups boiling water

1/2 cup rice flour
1/2 cup bean flour
1 teaspoon xanthan gum
1 cup granulated sugar
Cold water
Whipped topping
Almonds, sliced and toasted

HEAT sugar, water, and butter or margarine in large saucepan.

STIR and BOIL until thick. ADD boiling water.

MIX in a bowl flours, xanthan gum, sugar, and enough water to

make a paste. STIR into butter mixture.

BRING to a boil, then COOL. POUR into baked crust.

TOP with whipped topping and almonds.

Sometimes known as poor man's pie, here is . . .

AMISH SHOO-FLY PIE

(This recipe makes two pies.)

3/4 cup rice flour

3/4 cup bean flour

1 1/2 teaspoons xanthan gum

3 tablespoons oil

1/2 teaspoon nutmeg

1 teaspoon cinnamon

1 cup molasses

1/2 cup brown sugar

2 eggs

1 teaspoon baking soda
  dissolved in 1 cup hot water

2 9-inch Single Pie Crusts,
  unbaked (p. 152)

PREHEAT oven to 400°.

MIX flours, xanthan gum, oil, nutmeg, and cinnamon together until crumbly.

MIX in ANOTHER bowl molasses, sugar, eggs, and baking soda solution.

POUR half molasses mixture into one pastry-lined pie pan.

SPREAD half the flour mixture on top.

REPEAT with second pie crust.

BAKE at 400° for 10 minutes.

REDUCE heat to 350° and BAKE for 50 more minutes.

COOL.

Every creature on our farm appreciates, in its own way, our old King apple tree. It makes terrific cobbler.

APPLE COBBLER

2 pounds (about 6) apples
1 cup cold water
2 tablespoons cornstarch
1/2 teaspoon salt
1/3 cup granulated sugar

1 teaspoon cinnamon
1 teaspoon nutmeg
1 recipe Shortcake dough,
  unbaked (p. 16) or
  Sweet Dough (p. 154)

PREHEAT oven to 350°.

GREASE 9 x 12-inch baking dish.

PEEL, CORE, and SLICE apples and PLACE in greased baking dish.

MIX water and cornstarch in saucepan.

ADD salt, sugar, cinnamon, and nutmeg.

BOIL 5 minutes.

POUR over fruit.

ARRANGE shortcake dough or sweet dough strips over all.

BAKE at 350° for 20 minutes.

PEACH COBBLER

SUBSTITUTE 2 pounds of peaches for apples and ADD 1 teaspoon almond extract.

CHERRY COBBLER

1 cup cold water
2 tablespoons cornstarch
1/4 teaspoon cinnamon
1/4 teaspoon salt
1 pound sweet cherries

1/4 to 1/3 cup granulated sugar
1/2 teaspoon almond extract
1 recipe Shortcake batter,
*   unbaked (p. 16) or Emily's*
*   Rice Cakes batter (p. 206)*

PREHEAT oven to 350°. MIX water and cornstarch.

ADD cinnamon, salt, cherries, sugar, and almond extract.

BOIL 5 minutes. POUR into greased baking dish.

ARRANGE dough or SPREAD batter over the top.

BAKE at 350° for 20 minutes.

BERRY COBBLER

3 cups berries (boysenberries are great!)
Granulated sugar to taste (1/2 cup for boysenberries)
Few grains salt
1 tablespoon bean or rice flour or cornstarch
Butter or margarine
1 recipe Shortcake batter, unbaked (p. 16) or
*   Emily's Rice Cakes batter (p. 206)*

PREHEAT oven to 350°. BUTTER 8 x 8-inch baking dish.

MIX berries, sugar, salt, and flour or cornstarch.

SPREAD in buttered baking dish.

DOT with butter or margarine. SPREAD batter over the top.

BAKE at 350° for 20 to 25 minutes.

This is a fun look at how things were done in the past.
No pie plate to wash. Let us speak of . . .

CABBAGES AND KINGS . . . AND APPLE PIES

1 8-inch Single Pie Crust, unbaked (p. 152)
Tart apples (about 2), sliced
Granulated sugar or honey
1 tablespoon rice flour
1 teaspoon butter or margarine
1/2 teaspoon cinnamon
1 flat, outer, green cabbage leaf

PREHEAT oven to 350°.

LAY pie crust pastry on flat surface.

FILL one half with sliced apples.

ADD sugar or honey to taste.

SPRINKLE with rice flour.

DOT with butter or margarine.

SPRINKLE with cinnamon.

MOISTEN edges and FOLD empty half over apple half.

PINCH edges together.

PLACE pie on cabbage leaf.

PLACE on cookie sheet and PUT on bottom shelf of oven.

BAKE at 350° for 30 minutes.

A nicely different flavor!

In case you ever run into an elderberry . . .

ELDERBERRY PIE

3/4 cup brown sugar
1/4 cup rice flour
1/4 teaspoon cinnamon
1/4 teaspoon salt
2 cups ripe elderberries

Juice of 1/2 lemon
1 9-inch Single Pie Crust,
   unbaked (p. 152)
Additional pie dough or
   Sweet Dough (p. 154)

PREHEAT oven to 425°.

COMBINE sugar, flour, cinnamon, and salt.

ADD elderberries and lemon juice.

POUR berry mixture into pastry-lined pie pan.

COVER top of pie with strips of leftover pastry dough or
sweet dough.

BAKE at 425° for 10 minutes.

REDUCE heat to 325° and BAKE 30 minutes more.

You can reduce baking time by following the microwave instructions
on p. 155.

*Even if you've never liked rhubarb, you will want to try
this delectable combination of tastes.*

RHUBARB-BERRY CUSTARD PIE

1 10-inch Single Pie Crust,
  unbaked (p. 152)
1 tablespoon rice flour
1 1/4 cups granulated sugar
1/4 teaspoon nutmeg
4 beaten eggs
2 cups diced rhubarb
2 cups fresh raspberries or
  strawberries

Topping:
  1/4 cup rice flour
  1/4 cup sugar
  1/4 cup chopped almonds
  1/2 teaspoon cinnamon
  1/2 teaspoon nutmeg
  2 tablespoons butter
   or margarine

PREHEAT oven to 375°.

CUT a 12-inch square of tin foil with a 5-inch hole in the center.

MIX flour, sugar, nutmeg, and eggs in small bowl and BEAT well.

COMBINE rhubarb and berries and SPOON into pastry-lined pie pan.

ADD egg mixture.

COVER edges of pie shell with foil.

BAKE at 375° for 25 minutes.

REMOVE foil. BAKE 15 more minutes or until custard is set.

Topping:

COMBINE flour, sugar, almonds, cinnamon, and nutmeg.

CUT in butter with pastry cutter or fork until pieces are size of
small peas.

REMOVE pie from oven.

SPRINKLE topping mixture around outer edge of pie, leaving a
5-inch circle uncovered in center.

BAKE 5 more minutes.

In the old days, this pie was a delicious example of making do when fruit was expensive or hard to come by.

GREEN TOMATO PIE

8 medium green tomatoes
2 tablespoons lemon juice
  or vinegar
1/4 teaspoon salt
1 cup granulated sugar
1/4 teaspoon cinnamon

1 tablespoon oil
1 heaping tablespoon
  cornstarch
1/2 cup raisins
1 10-inch Double Pie Crust,
  unbaked (p. 152)

PREHEAT oven to 350°.

WASH tomatoes, REMOVE only stems, and CHOP or GRIND.

PLACE in saucepan with enough water to barely cover.

COOK 15 minutes.

ADD lemon juice, salt, sugar, and cinnamon.

MIX oil and cornstarch in small bowl.

ADD 1 tablespoon hot tomato liquid.

STIR until it becomes a paste, then ADD to saucepan.

STIR constantly until thickened.

ADD raisins and SIMMER a few minutes.

FILL pastry-lined pie pan with tomato mixture.

COVER with second crust, CRIMP edges, and CUT 3 or 4 steam vents in top.

BAKE at 350° for 30 minutes.

PEACH CRUNCH

1 quart (about 6) peaches	*1/2 cup peach juice or water*
1 tablespoon + 1/2 cup	*2 teaspoons baking powder*
granulated sugar	*1/2 teaspoon salt*
1 tablespoon + 1 cup	*2 tablespoons butter or margarine*
rice flour	*1 egg, beaten*

PREHEAT oven to 400°.

PEEL and SLICE peaches into a 2-quart baking dish.

MIX 1 tablespoon sugar, 1 tablespoon flour, and juice or water.

POUR over peaches.

COMBINE in a bowl 1/2 cup sugar, 1 cup flour, baking powder, salt, butter or margarine, and egg.

SPRINKLE over peach mixture.

BAKE at 400° for about 10 minutes, until browned.

You can garnish this delectable pie with bananas, kiwi fruit, maraschino cherries, or whatever pleases you!

CHOCOLATE CREAM PIE

1 9-inch Single Pie Crust, baked (p. 152)
1 cup Chocolate Pudding Mix (p. 271)
2 tablespoons butter or margarine

1 teaspoon vanilla extract (see note)
2 cups non-dairy whipped topping (optional)

COMBINE pudding mix and milk in saucepan and COOK over medium heat.

STIR until mixture thickens and bubbles.

COOK 1 minute longer.

REMOVE from heat and STIR in butter or margarine and vanilla.

COOL slightly.

POUR into cool pie crust.

COVER with plastic wrap.

REFRIGERATE 2 to 3 hours.

TOP with whipped topping, if using.

*Cathy Ehle, of Clackamas, Ore., gave me this recipe from
her mother. I adapted it to be wheat-free and dairy-free.
It's perfect if you don't have the mix on hand.*

CHOCOLATE CREAM PIE 2

1 1/2 cups granulated sugar
1/4 teaspoon salt
2 tablespoons cornstarch
2 1/2 squares baking
　chocolate
2 1/4 cups rice, soy, or
　coconut milk

1 tablespoon rice flour
2 egg yolks (see note)
1 tablespoon butter
1 teaspoon vanilla extract
1 Single Pie Crust, baked
　(p. 152)

COMBINE sugar, salt, cornstarch, chocolate, milk, and flour in a
large saucepan and BRING to a boil.

BOIL about 1 minute.

STIR in egg yolks and COOK 1 minute more.

ADD butter and vanilla.

POUR into cool pie crust and REFRIGERATE.

Note: Also works well with egg substitute or with no eggs at all!

If sugar is a problem, this recipe may give you some ideas.
Friend Edythe Moss makes this wonderful pie for husband Mel.

SUGAR-FREE RASPBERRY PIE

2 cups fresh or frozen raspberries
1 1/2 cups water
4 tablespoons cornstarch
1 small package sugar-free raspberry gelatin
Low calorie sweetener
1 9-inch Single Pie Crust, baked (p. 152)

COMBINE water, cornstarch, and gelatin.

COOK in saucepan over medium heat until clear.

COOL, then ADD sweetener such as Equal or Sweet 'n Low to taste.

BEAT well.

ADD raspberries.

POUR into cool pastry shell.

This is the real thing, just like grandma used to make.

HOMEMADE MINCEMEAT PIE

(You need at least 3 days.)

1 1/2 pounds lean, boneless beef chuck
1/2 pound kidney suet (see note)
2 cups apple cider
1 cup dark brown sugar
1 large orange
1 large lemon
6 tart green apples, peeled
15 ounces (about 2 1/2 cups) seedless raisins
10 ounces (about 1 1/2 cups) currants
1/2 pound candied lemon
1/2 pound candied citron
1/2 pound candied orange
2 teaspoons cinnamon
1 teaspoon EACH cloves, allspice, and nutmeg
1 cup brandy (optional)
1 9-inch Double Pie Crust, unbaked (p. 152)

COVER beef with water and SIMMER until tender, about 2 hours.

DRAIN and COOL.

GRIND or process beef and suet and SET ASIDE.

HEAT cider and sugar until sugar is dissolved.

STIR in beef and suet and MIX well.

CUT orange, lemon, and apple into quarters and REMOVE any seeds.

PROCESS or GRIND until finely chopped.

COMBINE raisins, currants, lemon, citron, and candied orange with beef mixture.

COVER and SIMMER for 1 hour, STIRRING frequently.

STIR in cinnamon, cloves, allspice, nutmeg, and brandy, if using.

SIMMER uncovered until liquid is reduced.

POUR into four 1-quart jars and SEAL.

STORE in refrigerator at least 3 days so flavors mellow.

PREHEAT oven to 400°.

FILL a 9-inch pastry-lined pie pan with 3 cups mincemeat.

COVER with second crust, CRIMP edges, and CUT 3 or 4 steam vents in top.

BAKE at 400° for 35 to 40 minutes.

SERVE warm or cold.

Note: Kidney suet may be found in your grocery store meat department or butcher shop.

RAISIN PECAN PIE

2 eggs, separated
1 cup granulated sugar
1 teaspoon cinnamon
1 teaspoon cloves
1/2 cup chopped pecans

1/2 cup raisins
1 tablespoon melted butter
1 tablespoon vinegar
1 8-inch Single Pie Crust,
  unbaked (p. 152)

PREHEAT to 325°.

BEAT egg yolks in a medium bowl.

COMBINE sugar, cinnamon, and cloves and ADD to yolks.

ADD pecans, raisins, and butter.

BEAT egg whites in a separate bowl.

FOLD into pecan mixture. ADD vinegar.

POUR into pastry-lined pie pan.

BAKE at 325° about 30 minutes, until crust and top are browned.

BE WATCHFUL because it burns easily. COOL before cutting.

OLD FASHIONED PUMPKIN PIE

3 eggs
2/3 cup brown sugar
3/4 cup water or milk
1 1/2 cups canned or
   cooked pumpkin,
   drained and mashed
1/4 teaspoon salt
1/2 teaspoon ginger

1 teaspoon nutmeg
1/4 teaspoon cloves
2 teaspoons cinnamon
1/2 teaspoon allspice
1 tablespoon hot water
1 8-inch Single Pie Crust,
   unbaked (p. 152)

PREHEAT oven to 425°.

BEAT eggs until light and creamy.

STIR in sugar, water or milk, pumpkin, and salt.

MIX ginger, nutmeg, cloves, cinnamon, and allspice with hot water
in another bowl, and ADD to egg mixture.

POUR into pastry-lined pie pan.

BAKE at 425° for 15 minutes.

REDUCE heat to 300° and BAKE for 40 minutes or until
custard sets.

Add the Praline Topping (see recipe on the next page) for a special
treat.

PRALINE TOPPING

2 tablespoons butter
1/2 cup light brown sugar, firmly packed
1/3 cup chopped pecans

MELT butter in small saucepan.

REMOVE from heat and STIR in brown sugar and pecans.

SPRINKLE evenly over pie.

PLACE praline-topped pie under broiler heat for 1 minute or until bubbly.

WATCH CAREFULLY so mixture does not burn.

SERVE warm.

IMPOSSIBLE PUMPKIN PIE

1/2 cup Biscuit Mix (p. 14)
3/4 cup granulated sugar
2 tablespoons butter or margarine
13 ounces evaporated milk or non-dairy creamer

2 eggs
2 cups (16 ounces) pumpkin
2 1/2 teaspoons pumpkin pie spice or 2 teaspoons allspice
2 teaspoons vanilla extract

PREHEAT oven to 350°. GREASE 9 or 10-inch pie pan.

BEAT all ingredients until smooth, in blender on high for 1 minute or by hand for 2 minutes. POUR into pie pan.

BAKE for 50 to 60 minutes, until knife inserted in center comes out clean. COOL before serving.

IMPOSSIBLE CHOCOLATE PIE

1/2 cup Biscuit Mix (p. 14)
1/2 cup granulated sugar
4 eggs
2 cups milk or water
3 tablespoons soft butter or
  margarine

4 tablespoons cocoa
1 teaspoon vanilla extract
1 teaspoon almond extract
1 teaspoon cinnamon
1 cup flaked coconut

PREHEAT oven to 325°.

GREASE 9-inch round baking pan.

COMBINE all ingredients except coconut in processor or blender.

PROCESS for 1 minute.

POUR into pan.

SPRINKLE coconut on top.

BAKE at 325° for 40 to 45 minutes.

COOL on wire rack.

CHILL.

IMPOSSIBLE FRENCH APPLE PIE

6 cups apples,
  sliced and peeled
1 1/4 teaspoons cinnamon
1/4 teaspoon nutmeg
1 cup brown sugar
3/4 cup milk or water
1/2 cup Biscuit Mix (p. 14)
2 eggs
2 tablespoons butter or
  margarine

Streusel Topping:
2/3 cup Biscuit Mix (p. 14)
1/2 cup nuts
2 tablespoons butter or
  margarine
1/4 cup brown sugar

PREHEAT oven to 325°.

GREASE 10-inch pie pan.

MIX apples, cinnamon, and nutmeg and POUR into pan.

BEAT sugar, milk or water, biscuit mix, eggs, and butter or margarine until smooth, in food processor for 15 seconds or by hand for 1 minute.

COMBINE streusel topping ingredients.

SPRINKLE pie with topping.

BAKE for 55 to 60 minutes, until knife inserted in center comes out clean.

LEMON MERINGUE PIE

*4 tablespoons cornstarch
(see note)*
*4 tablespoons rice flour
(see note)*
1/2 teaspoon salt
1 1/2 cups granulated sugar
1 1/2 cups boiling water
*1 tablespoon butter or
margarine*

*1/4 teaspoon grated
lemon rind*
1/3 cup lemon juice
4 egg yolks (reserve whites)
*1 9-inch Single Pie Crust,
baked (p. 152)*
*Foolproof Meringue
(see recipe on next page)*

MIX cornstarch, flour, salt, and sugar in top of double boiler.

ADD boiling water.

COOK and STIR over direct heat until mixture boils.

SET again in top of double boiler, COVER, and COOK 20 minutes.

ADD butter or margarine, lemon rind and juice, and egg yolks.

COOK and STIR until thick.

COOL (most important!).

MAKE meringue (see recipe below).

POUR cooled lemon mixture into cool pie crust.

SPOON meringue on top, SPREADING to touch edges.

BAKE at 425° about 5 minutes, until lightly browned.

Note: If you like a softer filling, reduce the flour and cornstarch.

FOOLPROOF MERINGUE

1 tablespoon cornstarch	*1/4 teaspoon cream of tartar*
2 tablespoons cold water	*4 egg whites*
1/2 cup boiling water	*1/3 cup sugar*

PREHEAT oven to 425°.

MIX cornstarch and cold water in small saucepan.

STIR in boiling water.

COOK over medium heat, STIRRING constantly until thickened, about 2 minutes.

REMOVE from heat and COOL (very important).

ADD cream of tartar to egg whites.

BEAT until soft peaks form.

ADD sugar gradually and CONTINUE beating.

ADD cornstarch mixture all at once.

BEAT until well blended.

SPREAD over pie.

BAKE meringue at 425° about 5 minutes, until lightly browned.

BERRY CRISP

4 cups blueberries or apples (see note)
1/3 cup granulated sugar
2 teaspoons lemon juice, if using berries
1/2 cup butter
2/3 cup brown sugar
2/3 cup oat or rice flour
1 1/2 cups uncooked quick oats

PREHEAT oven to 375°.

GREASE 9 x 12-inch, deep baking dish.

PUT berries in baking dish.

SPRINKLE with granulated sugar and lemon juice, if using.

CREAM butter and brown sugar.

ADD flour and oats.

SPREAD over berries.

BAKE at 375° for 40 minutes

OR

MICROWAVE on high for 15 minutes.

Note: A combination of 3 cups pears and 1 cup cranberries is a good option. Or combine 4 cups peaches with 1 teaspoon cinnamon.

Grandma Irene was famous for this recipe, although it was her mother's. She was often invited to dinner and asked to bring . . .

APPLE CHARLOTTE

Butter or shortening, divided
2 tablespoons + 1/4 cup brown sugar
1 Double Pie Crust, unbaked (p. 152)
5 or 6 green cooking apples, sliced
1/2 cup raisins
1/4 cup granulated sugar
1 teaspoon cinnamon
5 dabs butter or margarine

PREHEAT oven to 325°.

SPREAD thin layer of butter or shortening over only the bottom of 2-quart casserole.

SPRINKLE brown sugar in thin layer over bottom.

LINE casserole with layer of pastry as you would a pie pan.

FILL with apples.

LAYER raisins, 1/4 cup brown sugar, granulated sugar, and cinnamon.

DOT with 5 dabs butter or margarine.

COVER with second pastry.

BAKE at 325° for 1 hour 20 minutes, until top is browned.

TURN upside down on plate at once.

Cakes

*SOONER OR LATER WE ALL
DISCOVER THAT THE IMPORTANT
MOMENTS IN LIFE ARE
NOT THE ADVERTISED ONES,
NOT THE BIRTHDAYS, THE
GRADUATIONS, THE WEDDINGS,
NOT THE GREAT GOALS ACHIEVED. THE
REAL MILESTONES ARE LESS PREPOSSESS-
ING. THEY COME TO THE DOOR OF MEMORY
UNANNOUNCED, STRAY DOGS THAT AMBLE
IN,
SNIFF AROUND A BIT, AND SIMPLY NEVER
LEAVE. OUR LIVES ARE MEASURED BY
THESE.*

—Susan B. Anthony
  (grandniece of Susan B.)

(I remember the man who brought me eggs
on Thursdays!)

A time saver . . .

CAKE MIX

4 cups rice flour	1 tablespoon salt
4 cups bean flour	8 teaspoons xanthan gum
2 tablespoons baking soda	6 cups granulated sugar

COMBINE all ingredients in large bowl. STIR until blended.
DIVIDE into 6 packages.
STORE in one tightly sealed container in cool dry place. USE within
10 weeks.

Yield: about 6 cakes

VERY CHOCOLATE (SNACK) CAKE

2 1/4 cups Cake Mix (see recipe above)	1/3 cup vegetable oil
2 tablespoons unsweetened cocoa powder	1 teaspoon vanilla extract
3/4 cup water	1/2 cup semisweet chocolate chips
1 egg	1/2 cup chopped nuts

PREHEAT oven to 350°.
COMBINE cake mix and cocoa in ungreased 8 x 8-inch baking pan.
COMBINE water, egg, oil, and vanilla in medium bowl.
STIR into cocoa mixture until smooth and blended.
SPRINKLE chocolate chips and nuts evenly over batter.
BAKE at 350° for 30 to 40 minutes.

Yield: 9 servings

So good on spice cake or ginger cake . . .

BROILED COCONUT TOPPING

4 tablespoons butter or
   margarine
1/4 cup packed
   brown sugar

2 tablespoons milk or water
1/2 teaspoon vanilla extract
1/2 cup shredded coconut
1/2 cup chopped nuts

MELT butter in saucepan. STIR in remaining ingredients.

Yield: covers one 8 x 8-inch cake

OLD TIME GINGERBREAD

1/2 cup brown sugar
1/2 cup lard or shortening
1 cup dark molasses
1 egg, beaten
1 teaspoon baking soda
1 tablespoon chocolate or
   cocoa

1 1/8 cups rice flour
1 1/8 cups bean flour
2 teaspoons xanthan gum
1/2 teaspoon salt
1 tablespoon ginger
1 cup boiling water

PREHEAT oven to 325°. GREASE well 8 x 8 x 2-inch pan.

CREAM sugar, lard or shortening, and molasses in medium bowl.

ADD egg and MIX well.

SIFT dry ingredients in another bowl and ADD to sugar mixture.

MIX well. ADD hot water and MIX again.

POUR into greased pan.

BAKE at 325° for 60 to 70 minutes.

GINGERBREAD

2 1/2 cups Cake Mix (p. 184)	2 eggs
4 teaspoons baking powder	1 cup water
1 tablespoon ginger	2/3 cup molasses
1 teaspoon cinnamon	Whipped cream (optional)
1/4 teaspoon cloves	
1/2 cup butter or margarine	

PREHEAT oven to 325°.

GREASE and FLOUR 8 x 8 x 2-inch pan.

SIFT together dry ingredients in large mixing bowl.

MELT butter and BEAT with eggs and water.

ADD butter mixture to dry ingredients and STIR well.

ADD molasses and STIR well.

TURN into greased and floured pan.

BAKE at 325° for 60 minutes.

SERVE warm with whipped cream, if desired.

Broiled Coconut Topping is great on this cake.

SPICE CAKE

3/4 cup uncooked quick oats
1 1/4 cups boiling water
1 egg
1/3 cup vegetable oil
1 teaspoon cinnamon
1/2 teaspoon ground nutmeg

1 teaspoon vanilla extract
2 1/4 cups Cake Mix (p. 184)
1/2 cup chopped nuts
1/2 cup raisins
Broiled Coconut Topping
   (p. 185)

PREHEAT oven to 350°.

GREASE 8 x 8 x 2-inch pan.

COMBINE oats and boiling water and SET ASIDE.

COMBINE egg, oil, cinnamon, nutmeg, and vanilla.

STIR into softened oats mixture.

ADD cake mix.

ADD nuts and raisins and MIX.

POUR into greased pan.

BAKE at 325° for 45 minutes.

SPREAD ON topping immediately after baking.

PLACE cake in oven 3 inches below broiling element.

BROIL about 2 minutes until bubbly.

This is a wonderfully moist cake that freezes well.

FLOURLESS POUND CAKE

1 pound pecans	*1 pound (2 cups) granulated*
10 eggs, separated	*sugar*

PREHEAT oven to 250°. GREASE large tube pan.

GRIND nuts finely in food processor or blender, and SET ASIDE.

BEAT egg yolks until lemon-colored and very thick.

ADD sugar and nuts and STIR until well mixed. SET ASIDE.

BEAT egg whites until stiff.

FOLD 1/4 whites into nut mixture.

FOLD in remaining whites thoroughly.

POUR into tube pan.

BAKE at 250° to 300° for about 1 hour.

Good served with whipped cream or non-dairy topping.

ANOTHER CHOCOLATE CAKE

3 cups Biscuit Mix (p. 14)	*3 tablespoons cocoa*
3/4 cup water	*1 teaspoon vanilla extract*
2 eggs	*1 cup granulated sugar*

PREHEAT oven to 350°. GREASE 8 x 8 x 2-inch pan.

MIX all ingredients in large bowl. POUR into greased pan.

BAKE at 350° for 30 minutes.

This recipe came from a '50s out-of-print and untraceable cook-book, where it was called Old Joe Cake! Because in the '90s that is not politically correct, we call it . . .

PC CHOCOLATE CAKE

1 cup brown sugar
1 cup granulated sugar
1/2 cup lard
1 cup rice milk or water
1/2 cup cocoa, mixed with
   1/2 cup boiling water

1 teaspoon baking soda
1 teaspoon vanilla extract
1 1/2 cups rice flour
1 1/2 cups bean flour
3 teaspoons xanthan gum
Dash salt

PREHEAT oven to 325°.

MIX sugars and lard in large bowl.

ADD milk or water.

MIX cocoa liquid and baking soda and ADD to mixture.

ADD vanilla, flours, xanthan gum, and salt.

POUR into baking pan.

BAKE at 325° about 60 minutes.

CHOCOLATE PUDDING CAKE

1 cup Biscuit Mix (p. 14)
1 cup + 1/2 cup
* granulated sugar*
3 tablespoons + 1/3 cup
* unsweetened cocoa*

1/2 cup milk or water
1 teaspoon vanilla extract
1 2/3 cups hot water
Powdered sugar (optional)

PREHEAT oven to 325°.

GREASE 8-inch square baking pan.

MIX biscuit mix, 1 cup sugar, and 3 tablespoons cocoa in pan.

STIR in milk or water and vanilla.

SPRINKLE 1/3 cup cocoa and 1/2 cup sugar over mixture.

POUR hot water over top.

BAKE at 325° for 50 minutes or until top is firm.

DUST with powdered sugar, if using.

Yield: 6 servings

*Young son Neal made this cake for Dr. Harms, the veterinarian,
who loaned him a Hampshire ram to court the ladies in
Neal's flock of sheep.*

PINEAPPLE UPSIDEDOWN CAKE

*1 cup brown sugar
  firmly packed
1/2 cup butter or
  margarine
1 20-ounce can sliced
  pineapple, drained*

*3 cups Biscuit Mix (p. 14)
1 1/2 cups milk or water
1 1/3 cups granulated sugar
  or 1 cup honey
3 eggs, slightly beaten
1 1/2 teaspoons vanilla extract*

PREHEAT oven to 350°.

BUTTER one 13 x 9-inch pan or two 8-inch square pans.

COMBINE brown sugar and butter or margarine and PAT into
bottom of pan(s).

PLACE pineapple evenly over sugar mixture.

COMBINE biscuit mix and sugar or honey in large bowl.

COMBINE milk or water, eggs, and vanilla in small bowl.

ADD half milk mixture to dry ingredients.

BEAT 2 minutes until smooth.

ADD remaining milk mixture and BEAT 2 to 3 minutes.

SPREAD over pineapple.

BAKE 1 hour or until center springs back when touched.

COOL 10 minutes.

TURN over onto serving plate.

UPSIDEDOWN CAKE

Fresh or canned fruit
  (pineapple, peaches, etc.),
  sliced (see note)
1/3 cup brown sugar
1 tablespoon frozen orange
  juice concentrate, thawed

2 tablespoons butter
1/4 teaspoon cinnamon
1/4 cup chopped nuts
1 recipe Shortcake batter,
  unbaked (see p. 16)

PREHEAT oven to 350°.

GREASE 8 x 8-inch baking pan.

SPREAD sliced fruit in pan.

MIX brown sugar, juice, butter, cinnamon, and nuts.

SPREAD over fruit.

POUR shortcake batter over all.

BAKE at 350° for 25 minutes.

Note: Prepare enough fruit to cover bottom of your pan.

Especially good in your Cinnamon Raisin Stuffing . . .
if there is any left over!

EGGLESS, MILKLESS, BUTTERLESS CAKE

2 cups brown sugar
2 cups + 1 teaspoon hot water
2 tablespoons shortening
1 teaspoon salt
1 cup seedless raisins
1 teaspoon baking soda

1 teaspoon cinnamon
1 teaspoon cloves
1 1/2 cups rice flour
1 1/2 cups bean flour
3 teaspoons xanthan gum

PREHEAT oven to 325°.

GREASE two loaf pans.

BOIL together sugar, 2 cups water, shortening, salt, and raisins.

COOL until cold.

DISSOLVE baking soda in 1 teaspoon hot water.

ADD flours, cinnamon, cloves, xanthan gum, and baking soda solution to sugar mixture.

DIVIDE into two loaf pans.

BAKE at 325° for about 45 minutes.

Yield: 2 loaves

This cake will stay moist for quite some time.

*Ed's secretary brought this recipe into the bank one day.
It's awfully good! (I changed the wheat part.)*

CARROT CAKE

3/4 cup bean flour
3/4 cup rice flour
1/2 cup potato flour (see note)
2 teaspoons xanthan gum
2 teaspoons baking soda
1/2 teaspoon salt
2 teaspoons cinnamon
1/4 teaspoon nutmeg

1 1/2 cups cooking oil
4 eggs
1 1/2 cups honey
2 cups grated carrots
1 8-ounce can crushed
    pineapple, well drained
1 cup chopped walnuts
1 teaspoon vanilla extract

MIX together dry ingredients.

BEAT oil, eggs, and honey 3 minutes in another bowl.

ADD to flour mixture. ADD remaining ingredients.

POUR into 9 x 13-inch pan.

BAKE at 325° for 65 to 70 minutes. COOL.

SPREAD Cream Cheese Frosting (see recipe below) on cool cake.

Note: Instead of potato flour, increase rice flour by 1/2 cup.

CREAM CHEESE FROSTING

4 ounces cream cheese, softened
1/4 cup butter
2 teaspoons fresh lemon juice or
    frozen orange juice concentrate, thawed

1/2 teaspoon grated lemon
    or orange peel
1 cup powdered sugar

CREAM together butter and cream cheese.

Gradually ADD juice, lemon or orange peel, and sugar and BLEND.

Yield: enough for one 9 x 13-inch cake

This wonderful cake won a first place ribbon at the Clackamas County (Ore.) Fair in the summer of 1990. I was thrilled!

CHOCOLATE ZUCCHINI CAKE

1 cup rice flour
1 1/4 cups bean flour
2 teaspoons xanthan gum
1/2 cup cocoa
1 tablespoon baking powder
1 1/2 teaspoons baking soda
1 teaspoon salt
1 teaspoon cinnamon

3/4 cup butter, softened
2 cups granulated sugar
3 eggs
2 teaspoons vanilla extract
2 teaspoons orange peel
2 cups shredded zucchini
  (see note)
1/2 cup milk or water
1 cup chopped nuts

PREHEAT oven to 325°.

GREASE and FLOUR tube or loaf pan.

COMBINE flours, xanthan gum, cocoa, baking powder, baking soda, salt, and cinnamon and SET ASIDE.

CREAM butter and sugar.

ADD eggs one at a time, along with vanilla, orange peel, and zucchini.

STIR in, alternately, flour mixture and milk or water.

ADD nuts.

POUR batter into greased and floured pan.

BAKE at 325° about 1 1/2 hours.

COOL in oven 30 minutes with oven door open and heat turned off.

REMOVE from pan and COOL completely.

FROST if desired.

Note: Adding vegetables such as squash, pumpkin, and carrots gives moistness and structure to a wheat-free cake.

One sunny Monday I brought this toffee meringue to the folks at the library. I wanted to cheer them up because they couldn't be outside in the beautiful sunshine.

TOO BAD IT'S MONDAY CAKE

(You will need additional time.)
9 egg whites
1 teaspoon vanilla extract
1 teaspoon white wine vinegar
1 3/4 cups powdered sugar

Topping:
1 pint whipping cream OR
4 cups non-dairy
   whipped topping
6 1 1/4-ounces chocolate-
   covered toffee bars (Skor or
   Heath), chopped and divided

PREHEAT oven to 275°.

BEAT egg whites with electric mixer until soft peaks form.

BEAT in vanilla and vinegar until well blended.

GRADUALLY add sugar, and BEAT until peaks are stiff and glossy.

LINE 1 or 2 cookie sheets with brown paper.

TRACE two 9-inch circles on paper.

DIVIDE and SPREAD meringue mixture over both circles.

BAKE 1 hour. TURN off heat. DO NOT OPEN OVEN DOOR!

LET stand in oven 2 hours or until cool.

ASSEMBLE immediately when cool.

WHIP cream, if using, with electric mixer until soft peaks form. You should have 4 cups.

PUT 1/2 whipped topping in separate bowl.

FOLD in 4 chopped toffee bars.

REMOVE 1 meringue from pan to serving plate.

SPREAD with toffee mixture.

PLACE remaining meringue on top of toffee mixture.

SPREAD with plain whipped topping.

GARNISH with 2 chopped toffee bars.

REFRIGERATE 8 hours or overnight.

Yield: 12 servings

If you must avoid eggs, try this cake.

CIDER CAKE

1/2 cup butter	1 1/2 teaspoons baking soda
2 cups granulated sugar	1 teaspoon cinnamon
1 1/2 cups rice flour	1 teaspoon cloves or allspice
1 1/2 cups bean flour	3 teaspoons xanthan gum
1/2 cup arrowroot or	1 1/2 cups cider
tapioca flour	3 1/2 cups chopped raisins

PREHEAT oven to 325°.

GREASE bundt or tube pan.

CREAM butter and sugar.

COMBINE in another bowl flours, baking soda, cinnamon, cloves or allspice, and xanthan gum.

ADD to butter mixture alternately with cider, BEATING well.

ADD raisins and MIX well.

POUR into greased pan.

BAKE at 325° about 1 1/2 hours.

This wonderful dessert easily takes the place of a birthday or special occasion cake.

LEMON TORTE

(You will need additional time.)

4 egg whites
1 teaspoon vanilla extract
1/2 teaspoon cream of tartar
3/4 cup + 2/3 cup
  granulated sugar
2 tablespoons sliced almonds
1 teaspoon unflavored gelatin
6 egg yolks, beaten
1/2 teaspoon grated
  lemon peel
1/3 cup lemon juice
2 tablespoons margarine
1/3 cup water
3/4 cup whipping cream
  or non-dairy whipped topping

Fruit Sauce (optional):
1 1/2 cups berries
1 tablespoon cornstarch
2 tablespoons granulated
  sugar

PREHEAT oven to 300°.

BEAT egg whites, vanilla, and cream of tartar with an electric mixer until soft peaks form.

ADD 3/4 cup sugar gradually and BEAT until peaks are stiff.

LINE 2 or 3 cookie sheets with brown paper.

DRAW 3 circles each about 7 inches in diameter on the paper.

DIVIDE and SPREAD meringue mixture over circles about 1 inch thick.

SPRINKLE almonds over 1 circle for top layer.

BAKE at 300° for 45 minutes.

TURN off oven. DO NOT OPEN OVEN DOOR.

ALLOW meringues to dry in oven 3 hours or overnight.

COMBINE in saucepan 2/3 cup sugar and gelatin.

ADD egg yolks, lemon peel, lemon juice, margarine, and water.

COOK and STIR until bubbly.

COOK 2 more minutes.

REMOVE from heat and COVER saucepan with wax paper.

COOL.

CHILL until mixture becomes more firm, about 4 hours.

WHIP cream, if using, until soft peaks form.

ADD whipped cream or non-dairy whipped topping to lemon mixture.

PUT 1 meringue on platter.

SPREAD half lemon mixture over it.

PLACE second meringue on top.

SPREAD remaining lemon mixture over it.

PLACE meringue with almonds on top.

COVER loosely with plastic wrap.

CHILL 6 hours or overnight.

To Make Fruit Sauce:

COMBINE berries, cornstarch, and sugar in medium saucepan.

COOK about 2 minutes until bubbly.

COVER and CHILL.

AUSTRIAN CAKES

2 tablespoons butter or
  margarine
5 eggs at room
  temperature, separated
3 teaspoons granulated
  sugar, divided

Pinch salt
1/3 cup powdered sugar
1/4 cup rice flour
1 teaspoon vanilla extract
2 tablespoons cream sherry

PREHEAT oven to 350°.

MELT butter in 10-inch shallow baking dish or ovenproof skillet.

BEAT egg whites in medium bowl just until they form peaks.

SPRINKLE with 2 teaspoons granulated sugar.

BEAT whites until they are stiff but not dry.

BEAT egg yolks in large bowl with powdered sugar, about 1 minute.

STIR flour, salt, vanilla, sherry, and 1/4 egg whites into yolk mixture.

FOLD in remaining whites gently.

SPOON 6 mounds egg mixture into baking dish.

BAKE 10 to 12 minutes until lightly browned and still slightly soft.

SPRINKLE with 1 teaspoon granulated sugar.

Yield: 6 servings

This filling is so simple and so good!
The Australians call the finished meringue dessert Pavlova,
in honor of the celebrated ballerina, Anna Pavlova.

KIWI FILLING

1 cup chilled whipping cream (see note)
2 tablespoons granulated sugar (see note)
3 kiwis, peeled and sliced or
1 1/2 to 2 cups fresh strawberries, raspberries, or blueberries

COMBINE whipping cream and sugar and BEAT until stiff.

FROST top and sides of meringue (see recipe above).

ARRANGE kiwi slices or berries on top.

Note: If you substitute non-dairy whipped topping, omit sugar.

MERINGUE

(You will need additional time.)

3 egg whites   *1/2 teaspoon vanilla extract*
1/4 teaspoon cream of tartar   *3/4 cup granulated sugar*

PREHEAT oven to 325°.

LINE cookie sheet with brown paper.

TRACE a circle about 8 or 9 inches in diameter.

BEAT egg whites and cream of tartar until foamy. ADD vanilla.

BEAT in sugar, 1 tablespoon at a time, until stiff.

SPREAD within the circle 2 to 3 inches thick.

BAKE 1 1/2 hours. TURN off oven.

DO NOT OPEN OVEN DOOR. COOL in oven for 3 hours.

PUT meringue on platter. SPREAD kiwi filling (see recipe above) on meringue. CUT into wedges to serve.

APPLE CAKE

2 cups coarsely grated apples
3/4 cup honey or
   1 cup granulated sugar
1/2 teaspoon salt
1 teaspoon baking soda
1 teaspoon cinnamon
1/2 teaspoon nutmeg

1/4 cup oil
1/2 cup raisins
1 cup chopped nuts
3/4 cup rice flour
3/4 cup bean flour
1 teaspoon xanthan gum

PREHEAT oven to 325°. GREASE 8-inch square pan.

MIX all ingredients. POUR into greased pan.

BAKE at 325° for 60 minutes.

APPLESAUCE CAKE

3/4 cup bean flour
3/4 cup rice flour
1 1/2 teaspoons xanthan gum
1 cup granulated sugar
1 teaspoon baking soda
1/2 teaspoon salt
1/2 teaspoon cinnamon

1/4 teaspoon nutmeg
1/8 teaspoon cloves
1 tablespoon vinegar
6 tablespoons vegetable oil
1 teaspoon vanilla extract
3/4 cup applesauce
1/4 cup cold water

PREHEAT oven to 350°. GREASE 8-inch square pan.

MIX all ingredients. POUR into greased pan.

BAKE at 350° for 25 minutes.

Ann Wilkerson, from Bloomington, Ind., sent me her favorite cake recipe. I tried it and agree. Thank you, Ann!

APPLESAUCE RAISIN CAKE

2 cups ground uncooked
   quick oats (see note)
2/3 cup granulated sugar
1/2 teaspoon salt
1 teaspoon baking soda
2 teaspoons cinnamon

1/2 teaspoon nutmeg
1/4 cup oil
2 eggs
1 teaspoon vanilla extract
1 cup applesauce
1 cup raisins

PREHEAT oven to 350°.

GREASE 8-inch square baking pan.

COMBINE ground oats, sugar, salt, baking soda, cinnamon and nutmeg in large bowl.

ADD oil, eggs, and vanilla.

BEAT until smooth, about 2 minutes.

STIR in applesauce and raisins.

POUR batter into greased pan.

BAKE at 350° for 35 to 40 minutes.

COOL, COVER, and STORE 1 day before serving.

(I couldn't wait that long and tasted the cake when it was still warm . . . very nice!)

Ann uses a burnt sugar icing on this cake, but I like it just plain.

Note: You can grind oats in your food processor.

This recipe is a family tradition.
I make it every fall, all the while remembering "It's fruitcake
weather," from Truman Capote's story "A Christmas Memory."

DARK FRUITCAKE

1 1/2 pounds raisins
1 pound citron, orange, or
  lemon peel
3 to 4 pounds glacéd fruits
1/2 pound dates
2 cups chopped apples
1 pound walnuts
2 1/2 cups rice flour, divided
2 1/2 cups bean flour, divided
1 cup butter
2 cups brown sugar
7 eggs, separated
1 12-ounce jar apple or
  grape jelly

1 tablespoon cinnamon
1 tablespoon allspice
1 teaspoon cloves
1 teaspoon nutmeg
1 tablespoon baking powder
1/2 teaspoon baking soda
5 teaspoons xanthan gum
1 tablespoon rum extract
2 teaspoons vanilla extract
1/2 cup molasses
Corn syrup

PREHEAT oven to 250°.

GREASE two 10-inch tube pans and LINE with heavy brown paper
(see note).

SET ASIDE enough glacéd fruits for decorating tops of cakes.

CUT remaining fruits and nuts into small pieces.

DREDGE in 2 cups rice or bean flour.

CREAM butter and sugar in large bowl.

ADD one egg yolk at a time.

BEAT until smooth.

BLEND in jelly.

SIFT in another bowl remaining flour with cinnamon, allspice,
cloves, nutmeg, baking powder, baking soda, and xanthan gum.

ADD to butter mixture.

ADD rum, vanilla, and molasses and MIX well.

ADD fruits to butter mixture.

BEAT egg whites until stiff but not dry, and ADD to butter mixture.

FOLD into two tube pans.

PLACE shallow pan of water on bottom shelf of oven (see note).

BAKE at 250° for 3 1/2 to 4 hours, until inserted cake tester is moist but not doughy.

COOL cakes in pan.

BRUSH with corn syrup and DECORATE with reserved fruit about 30 minutes after cake is done.

Note: Lining pans with heavy brown paper and setting a pan of water on the bottom of oven should prevent excessive browning.

In 1851 Emily Dickinson wrote Sue Gilbert,
then teaching in Baltimore, mentioning how happy she was
to send rice cakes to her friend. This is her recipe.

EMILY'S RICE CAKES

1/2 cup butter
1 cup powdered sugar
2 eggs
1 cup rice flour
1 tablespoon milk mixed with
   1/4 teaspoon baking soda
1 teaspoon mace, or nutmeg, or both

PREHEAT oven to 350°.

GREASE 8-inch round pan.

CREAM butter.

ADD sugar to butter, and BLEND.

BEAT eggs in a separate bowl.

ADD eggs gently to butter mixture.

ADD remaining ingredients.

POUR into greased pan.

BAKE at 350° for 15 to 20 minutes.

"Rice cakes were usually saved to serve a guest who dropped in for tea. At 'handed teas,' everyone sat down as platters of food were passed. Such bounty sometimes served as supper." *Emily Dickinson Profile of the Poet as Cook*, by Nancy Harris Brose, 1946.

Thanks to instructor Jan Anderson who gave me this wonderful recipe. Emily's Rice Cakes started me experimenting with rice and other non-wheat flours.

I am indebted to Audrey Sinner for this deliciously moist cake.

OATMEAL CAKE

1 1/4 cups boiling water
1 cup uncooked quick oats
1/2 cup margarine
1 cup granulated sugar
1 cup packed brown sugar
 1 teaspoon vanilla extract
2 eggs
1 1/2 cups oat flour
1 teaspoon xanthan gum
1/2 teaspoon salt
1 teaspoon baking soda
3/4 teaspoon cinnamon
1/4 teaspoon nutmeg

Frosting:
 1/4 cup margarine or
  butter, melted
 1/2 cup firmly packed
  brown sugar
 3 tablespoons water
 1/3 cup chopped nuts
 3/4 cup shredded or flaked
  coconut

PREHEAT oven to 350°. GREASE well 8 x 8 x 2-inch pan.

POUR boiling water over oats, COVER and LET STAND for
20 minutes.

BEAT butter, gradually ADDING sugars, until fluffy.

BLEND in vanilla and eggs. ADD oat mixture and MIX well.

MIX together in another bowl flour, xanthan gum, salt, baking soda,
cinnamon, and nutmeg.

ADD to creamed mixture and MIX well.

POUR batter into greased pan.

BAKE at 350° for 50 to 55 minutes.

COMBINE all frosting ingredients.

SPREAD evenly over still-warm cake.

BROIL until frosting bubbles.

This delightful old recipe reminds me of a pound cake,
but it is made with cornstarch instead of flour.
Good with fruit toppings, frosted, or just plain.

SAND CAKE

1 cup butter or margarine	*5 eggs, separated*
1 teaspoon salt	*1 1/2 cups cornstarch*
1 cup granulated sugar	*1 teaspoon lemon extract*

PREHEAT oven to 350°.

GREASE 9 x 9-inch cake pan and LINE with greased brown paper.

COMBINE butter and salt until creamy.

ADD sugar 1 tablespoon at a time, MIXING well.

ADD egg yolks one at a time to butter mixture. BEAT after
each addition.

ADD cornstarch to butter mixture 1 tablespoon at a time.

STIR in lemon extract.

BEAT egg whites in another bowl until soft peaks form.

FOLD gently into batter.

POUR into greased and lined pan.

BAKE at 350° about 40 minutes, until light brown and toothpick
inserted comes out clean.

JAM CAKE

1/2 cup butter or cooking oil
1 cup granulated sugar
2 eggs, beaten
3/4 cup rice flour
3/4 cup bean flour
1 1/2 teaspoons xanthan gum
1/2 teaspoon baking soda
1/2 teaspoon cinnamon

1/2 teaspoon cloves
1/2 teaspoon nutmeg
1/2 teaspoon allspice
1/2 cup buttermilk
1/2 cup jam
1/2 cup chopped nuts
1/2 cup sliced citron

PREHEAT oven to 350°.

GREASE 8-inch square baking pan.

CREAM butter or oil and sugar.

ADD beaten eggs.

COMBINE in another bowl flours, xanthan gum, baking soda,
cloves, nutmeg, and allspice.

ADD egg mixture and buttermilk to flour mixture.

FOLD in jam, nuts, and citron.

POUR into greased pan.

BAKE at 350° for 45 minutes.

Yield: 12 servings

PASSOVER SPONGE CAKE

12 eggs, separated
Pinch salt
1 1/2 cups granulated sugar
2 tablespoons lemon juice
1 cup + 1 tablespoon
* potato starch*

PREHEAT oven to 325°.

LINE bottom of tube pan with brown paper.

BEAT egg whites until stiff.

ADD salt.

ADD sugar slowly, still beating.

COMBINE in another bowl egg yolks, lemon juice, and potato starch.

FOLD yolk mixture gently into egg whites.

POUR batter into pan.

BAKE at 325° for 1 hour 10 minutes. DO NOT OPEN OVEN DOOR while baking.

COOL cake upside down on wire rack.

UNMOLD by sliding a long serrated knife between cake and pan.

SERVE with fresh strawberries or other fruit.

PRUNE FLAN

(You will need additional time.)
1 pound pitted prunes
3 tablespoons brandy
5 tablespoons granulated
  sugar, divided
3 large eggs
4 tablespoons oat or rice flour
2 cups milk or water

SOAK prunes in brandy for at least 1 or 2 days.

PREHEAT oven to 375°.

BUTTER and FLOUR 10-inch baking dish with straight sides.

ADD 1 tablespoon sugar to prunes and COMBINE.

LAYER prunes in baking dish.

MIX eggs with 3 tablespoons sugar and BEAT until blended.

COMBINE with flour and ADD milk or water.

POUR mixture over prunes.

BAKE at 375 ° for 45 minutes.

REMOVE from oven when brown and bubbling.

SPRINKLE with remaining tablespoon sugar.

COOL and SERVE at room temperature.

A blue ribbon winner, this cake took Best of Show
at the Clackamas (Ore.) County Fair!

FUDGE TORTE

3/4 cup butter or margarine
6 tablespoons cocoa
1 cup granulated sugar,
    divided
2/3 cup ground blanched
    almonds
2 tablespoons rice flour

3 eggs, separated
2 tablespoons +
    a few drops water
Powdered sugar
Chocolate Glaze
    (see recipe below)

MELT butter in saucepan over low heat.

STIR in cocoa and 3/4 cup sugar and BLEND until smooth.

REMOVE from heat and COOL 5 minutes.

ADD almonds and flour.

BEAT in egg yolks, one at a time.

ADD 2 tablespoons water.

PREHEAT oven to 350°.

GREASE and FLOUR 9-inch square pan.

BEAT egg whites in a separate bowl until foamy.

ADD remaining 1/4 cup sugar slowly, BEATING until soft
peaks form.

FOLD chocolate mixture gently into egg whites.

POUR into greased and floured pan.

BAKE at 350° for 30 minutes or until cake tester comes out clean.

COOL 10 minutes (cake will settle slightly).

REMOVE from pan onto rack and COOL completely.

INVERT cake onto serving plate.

MIX powdered sugar with a few drops water.

SPREAD thin mixture onto cake top and sides and LET DRY.

SPREAD with chocolate glaze and DECORATE if you desire.

Yield: 8 to 10 servings

CHOCOLATE GLAZE

2 tablespoons butter or margarine
2 tablespoons cocoa
2 tablespoons water
1/2 teaspoon vanilla extract
1 cup powdered sugar

MELT butter or margarine in small saucepan over low heat.

ADD cocoa and water.

STIR constantly until thickened; do not boil.

REMOVE from heat and ADD vanilla.

ADD sugar gradually, BEATING until smooth.

A visit to Mary Witt down the road netted me this opinion on which version torte (dairy or non-dairy) to include: "Put both of them in." Tortes require very little flour and are easy to make.

THE DAIRY TORTE

1 cup sour cream	3/4 cup rice flour
1 cup granulated sugar	1/2 teaspoon xanthan gum
2 egg yolks	1 tablespoon butter or
1/4 teaspoon salt	margarine, melted
1/4 teaspoon baking soda	10 walnuts, chopped

PREHEAT oven to 300°.

GREASE an 8-inch or 9-inch cast-iron frying pan.

CUT a circle of wax or parchment paper to fit bottom.

GREASE and FLOUR paper and LAY in pan.

MIX sour cream, sugar, and egg yolks in large bowl.

MIX dry ingredients in separate bowl.

ADD dry ingredients to sour cream mixture.

ADD butter and nuts, and MIX well.

POUR into prepared pan.

BAKE at 300° about 20 minutes or until a knife inserted comes out clean.

COOL on rack 20 minutes.

TURN upside down and REMOVE cake.

REMOVE paper liner when cool enough to handle.

Mary actually chose this torte as her favorite,
without knowing it was dairy-free.

THE NON-DAIRY TORTE

Follow directions for Dairy Torte (see recipe above), but SUBSTI-TUTE 8 ounces tofu for sour cream, and ADD 1 teaspoon vanilla or almond extract.

BLEND tofu in processor or blender.

CRÈME FRAICHE

(You will need additional time.)

PUT 2 tablespoons buttermilk and 1 cup heavy cream in a jar,

COVER, and SHAKE until combined.

LET STAND in warm place until thickened, 12 to 14 hours.

STRAWBERRY TOFU TORTE

1 1/2 cups uncooked
  quick oats
1/2 cup finely
  chopped almonds
1/3 cup packed brown sugar
1/3 cup margarine, melted
1 14-ounce block firm or
  medium tofu
3 eggs

2/3 cup granulated sugar
2 teaspoons grated orange peel
2 tablespoons lemon juice
1 ripe banana
8 ounces strawberries,
  crushed and drained
  (see note)
Whipped topping or
  crushed fruit

PREHEAT oven to 350°.

GREASE bottom and sides of 10-inch pie or cheesecake pan.

COMBINE oats, almonds, sugars, and margarine and MIX well.

PRESS firmly to bottom and sides of pan. SET ASIDE.

PROCESS tofu lightly in food processor.

ADD eggs, sugar, orange peel, and lemon juice, and PROCESS.

ADD banana in chunks and PROCESS until smooth.

STIR in strawberries.

POUR into crust-lined pan.

BAKE at 350° for 45 to 50 minutes or until firm. COOL.

TOP with whipped topping or crushed fruit.

Note: Substitute blueberries or other favorite fruit for strawberries.
If using cherries, omit orange peel.

This wonderful fruit-filled pancake, a traditional French dessert from Limousin, is best when served warm.

CHERRY CLAFOUTIS

(You will need additional time.)

3 cups pitted sweet cherries
1/4 cup brandy
1/4 cup + 1 tablespoon rice flour
1/4 cup + 1 tablespoon bean flour
1/2 teaspoon xanthan gum
1 cup granulated sugar
Pinch salt

4 eggs
3 1/2 tablespoons unsalted butter or margarine, melted
1 1/2 teaspoons vanilla extract
Water or cherry juice
Powdered sugar
Crème Fraiche
(see p. 215)
or non-dairy whipped topping

SOAK cherries in brandy for at least 1 hour.

PREHEAT oven to 325°.

BUTTER a 10-inch pie pan.

COMBINE flours, xanthan gum, sugar, and salt in mixing bowl.

ADD eggs one at a time, MIXING gently with a fork.

ADD vanilla and MIX.

DRAIN cherries and COMBINE cherry juice with water to make 3/4 cup liquid.

PLACE cherries in bottom of pan.

STIR butter and cherry liquid into batter.

POUR batter over cherries.

BAKE at 325° for 35 minutes or until golden and set in the center.

COOL briefly and SPRINKLE with powdered sugar.

SERVE warm with crème fraîche or whipped topping.

*I found this recipe with some old cookbooks in a house on
Whidbey Island, Wash. where we spent Christmas 1992.
I adapted it to be wheat-free.*

TOPSEY TURVEY PUDDING

*1/2 cup rice flour
1/2 cup bean flour
1 teaspoon xanthan gum
2 teaspoons baking powder
1/4 teaspoon salt
1 cup granulated sugar,
    divided*

*1/8 cup oil or 1/4 cup
    shortening, softened
    (see note)
2/3 cup water
1 2/3 to 2 cups dark
    cherries, pitted,
1 cup cherry juice*

PREHEAT oven to 350°.

GREASE well 8-inch square baking dish or casserole.

SIFT together flours, xanthan gum, baking powder, salt, and
1/2 cup sugar.

ADD shortening and water.

BEAT until smooth.

POUR into casserole or baking dish.

PUT cherries on top.

COMBINE cherry juice and remaining 1/2 cup sugar.

POUR over cherries.

BAKE at 350° for 45 minutes.

Note: If you substitute oil for shortening, the cake will be a bit denser.

This wonderful Christmas plum pudding tastes like a fruitcake.

GRANDMA'S PLUM PUDDING

*2 slices wheat-free
  bread, cubed
1 cup milk or water
6 ounces beef suet, ground
1 cup brown sugar
2 eggs, beaten
1/4 cup orange juice
1 teaspoon vanilla extract
2 cups raisins
1 cup pitted dates, snipped*

*1/2 cup diced mixed
  candied fruits
1/2 cup chopped walnuts
1 cup rice flour
1 teaspoon xanthan gum
2 teaspoons cinnamon
1 teaspoon cloves
1 teaspoon mace
1 teaspoon baking soda
1/2 teaspoon salt*

GREASE a 2-quart mold.

SOAK bread in milk or water in large bowl and BEAT to break up.

STIR in suet, sugar, eggs, juice, and vanilla and SET ASIDE.

COMBINE in another bowl raisins, dates, candied fruits, and nuts, and SET ASIDE.

COMBINE in another bowl flour, xanthan gum, cinnamon, mace, baking soda, and salt.

ADD to fruit mixture and MIX well. STIR in bread-suet mixture.

POUR into mold. COVER with tinfoil and TIE securely.

BOIL water for steaming.

PLACE mold on rack or jar rings in large pot or canner.

ADD about 1 inch boiling water.

COVER and STEAM 4 hours. ADD more boiling water when needed.

COOL about 10 minutes. REMOVE from mold.

SERVE with hard sauce (p. 223) or any sweet, fruity sauce.

Wheat-free steamed puddings turn out so well!

STEAMED PUDDING

3 tablespoons melted butter,
  divided
1 cup pitted dates or
  3/4 cup raisins
2 medium carrots, grated
1 large potato, grated
1/2 cup chopped almonds
2 eggs
1/4 teaspoon salt
1 cup brown sugar

1 teaspoon vanilla extract
1 teaspoon baking soda
  mixed with
   2 tablespoons hot water
1/2 cup rice flour
1/3 cup bean flour
1 teaspoon xanthan gum
1 teaspoon cinnamon
1/2 teaspoon ground cloves

GREASE 2-quart mold with 1 tablespoon melted butter.

CUT dates in half lengthwise.

GRATE carrots and potato by hand or in processor.

COMBINE dates, carrots, potato, and nuts in large bowl.

COMBINE in another bowl eggs, salt, sugar, vanilla, and dissolved
baking soda.

ADD to date mixture.

COMBINE in another bowl flours, xanthan gum, cinnamon,
and cloves.

ADD to date mixture and STIR well.

TURN batter into greased mold.

POUR rest of melted butter over top of pudding.

COVER with lid or double thickness of foil tied securely.

BOIL water for steaming.

SET mold on rack or jar rings in deep kettle or canner with lid.

ADD boiling water until it reaches halfway up sides of mold.

COVER and STEAM 2 1/2 hours, KEEPING water boiling gently.

COOL pudding about 10 minutes.

REMOVE from mold.

SERVE with hard sauce (p. 223) flavored with whiskey, brandy, or cognac or with any sweet, fruity sauce.

For your steamed puddings . . .

APRICOT GLAZE

2 cups apricot preserves	1 tablespoon brandy

WARM preserves in saucepan over low heat until melted.

STIR in brandy.

PROCESS in blender or food processor or PRESS through fine sieve.

USE a pastry brush to BRUSH over entire pudding.

*Brought up to date for the microwave, here's a very rich raisin
pudding from another old recipe.*

A DICKENS OF AN ENGLISH PLUM PUDDING

2 1/2 cups raisins
1/4 cup finely ground suet
3 tablespoons fresh
bread crumbs
2 tablespoons rice flour
3 tablespoons mixed
glacéd fruit
2 tablespoons brown sugar

1 tablespoon molasses
1/4 teaspoon cinnamon
1/4 teaspoon nutmeg
1/4 teaspoon baking powder
1 egg, beaten
1/2 cup beer
4 tablespoons brandy,
divided

GREASE a 4-cup glass or porcelain mold.

COMBINE all ingredients except 2 tablespoons brandy.

SPOON batter into mold.

COVER with plastic wrap.

MICROWAVE on medium 10 to 14 minutes or until a toothpick
inserted comes out clean. ROTATE mold several times if you do not
have a rotating device.

SET on counter and COOL 15 minutes.

TURN onto serving dish.

POUR remaining 2 tablespoons brandy into 1-cup glass measure.

MICROWAVE on high 15 seconds and POUR over pudding.

LIGHT with match immediately and SERVE.

SERVE warm or cold with hard sauce (see recipe below) or any well-
flavored sauce.

It's nearly impossible to make a real hard sauce without butter, so for those who can tolerate a little butter, here's a basic sauce for steamed puddings. (The British know how to warm your heart on a cold day!)

HARD SAUCE

1/3 cup butter, softened
1 cup powdered sugar
1/2 teaspoon vanilla extract
Brandy or whiskey (optional + see note)

CREAM softened butter thoroughly.

BEAT in powdered sugar gradually.

ADD vanilla drop by drop.

ADD 1 teaspoon liquor drop by drop, if using.

If sauce separates, ADD 1 teaspoon boiling water drop by drop.

SERVE at room temperature or chilled.

Note: Being allergic to wheat means you have to avoid whiskey and maybe all grain alcohol drinks, but you might be able to have brandy. If you are not sure, check with your doctor or nutritionist.

For liquor, you can substitute:

2 tablespoons strong coffee and 2 teaspoons cocoa OR
2 tablespoons orange juice and 2 tablespoons grated
  orange rind OR
1 tablespoon lemon juice and 1 tablespoon grated
  lemon rind.

These doughnuts are wonderfully good! If you have to substitute
for the buttermilk, the doughnuts will be denser and heavier,
but still very tasty.

SINFULLY GOOD DOUGHNUTS

(Must be started a day in advance.)

2 eggs
1 cup granulated sugar
1 cup mashed
potatoes (about 2 medium)
5 tablespoons lard, melted
1 cup buttermilk or 1 cup
soft tofu, liquified in
blender
2 teaspoons vanilla extract
1 1/2 cups bean flour

1 1/2 cups rice flour
3 teaspoons xanthan gum
3 teaspoons baking powder
1 1/2 teaspoons nutmeg
1 teaspoon baking soda
2 1/4 teaspoons
cream of tartar
1/2 teaspoon salt
2 quarts vegetable oil
Powdered sugar (see note)

BEAT eggs until frothy.

ADD sugar and BLEND well.

STIR in potatoes, lard, buttermilk or tofu, and vanilla.

SIFT dry ingredients except powdered sugar and ADD to
potato mixture.

MIX just until flour is completely moistened.

COVER dough and REFRIGERATE overnight.

PREHEAT oil in fryer or Dutch oven to 370°.

ROLL 1/2 dough on heavily-floured surface to 1/2 inch thick.
REFRIGERATE other half.

CUT out doughnuts with heavily floured doughnut cutter or
pineapple cutter.

SLIDE doughnuts into hot fat with metal spatula and FRY until
golden brown on underside, 1 to 2 minutes.

TURN carefully and FRY 1 minute.

REMOVE from fat and DRAIN on paper towels.

FRY doughnut holes and DRAIN on paper towels.

COOL, then SHAKE doughnuts with powdered sugar in paper sack.

Note: Doughnuts store better unsugared.

Yield: 24 doughnuts

I would never buy a doughnut maker if I could eat store-bought ones, but with the new Teflon-coated products we can indulge because no "fat" is involved . You may even want to double the recipe!

DOUGHNUTS

1 recipe Emily's Rice Cakes batter, unbaked (p. 206)

ADD 1/2 cup water. MIX well.

FILL doughnut maker 3/4 full of batter.

CLOSE machine and COOK for 5 to 7 minutes.

Yield: 7 doughnuts

These are wonderful frosted and dipped in chopped nuts.

MISSISSIPPI MUD CAKE

4 eggs
1/2 cup margarine,
  melted
3 cups Brownie Mix
  (p. 234)
1 teaspoon vanilla extract

2 cups chopped nuts
1 cup flaked coconut
7 ounces marshmallow
  creme
Chocolate Icing
  (see recipe below)

PREHEAT oven to 325°.

GREASE and FLOUR 13 x 9-inch baking pan.

BEAT eggs until foamy.

ADD margarine.

ADD brownie mix and BLEND well.

STIR in vanilla, nuts, and coconut.

POUR into prepared pan.

BAKE about 30 minutes, until edges separate from pan.

SPREAD on marshmallow creme while cake is still hot.

COOL. FROST with chocolate icing (see recipe below).

CHOCOLATE ICING

1/2 cup butter, melted
6 tablespoons water

4 tablespoons unsweetened cocoa
1 pound powdered sugar

COMBINE butter, water, and cocoa in large bowl.

ADD powdered sugar gradually, BEATING until smooth.

Although this is wheat-free, it is not dairy-free.
There is no substitute for real cheese.

ALMOND CHEESECAKE

1 1/2 uncooked cups quick oats
1/2 cup finely chopped almonds
1/3 cup packed brown sugar
1/3 cup margarine, melted
16 ounces cream cheese,
* softened*
1/2 cup + 2 tablespoons
* granulated sugar*

1 teaspoon almond extract,
* divided*
3 eggs
2 cups sour cream, divided
Garnishes (optional):
* Whipped cream*
* Orange slices*
* Almonds*

PREHEAT oven to 350°.

GREASE bottom and sides of 9-inch springform pan.

MIX WELL oats, almonds, brown sugar, and margarine.

PRESS firmly onto bottom and 1 1/2 inches up sides of pan.

BAKE 18 minutes. COOL.

BEAT cheese, 1/2 cup granulated sugar, and 1/2 teaspoon almond
extract at medium speed of mixer until fluffy.

ADD eggs one at a time, BEATING well after each.

STIR in 1 cup sour cream. POUR into prepared crust.

BAKE at 350° for 50 minutes or until center is set.

MIX remaining granulated sugar, almond extract, and sour cream,
and SPREAD over cheesecake.

CONTINUE baking 10 minutes.

LOOSEN cake from rim of pan, COOL, and REMOVE rim.

CHILL. ADD garnishes, if using.

Yield: 16 servings

Another old-fashioned recipe . . .

APPLE ROLL

About 2 medium apples,
  peeled and cored
1 cup rice flour
1 cup bean flour
2 teaspoons xanthan gum
1/2 teaspoon salt
2 tablespoons sugar
4 teaspoons baking powder

1 tablespoon lard
1 egg
1/2 cup rice or soy milk
Cinnamon

Syrup:
2 cups granulated sugar
1 cup water

PREHEAT oven to 350°.

GREASE cookie sheet.

CUT apples into thin slices and SET ASIDE.

COMBINE rest of ingredients except cinnamon to form dough.

ROLL out dough into oval shape to thickness of pie crust.

COVER dough with apple slices.

SPRINKLE with cinnamon and ROLL up lengthwise.

CUT into pieces about 2 inches long. PLACE on greased
cookie sheet.

COOK sugar in water until it dissolves to make syrup.

POUR syrup over pieces.

BAKE at 350° for about 30 minutes.

Cookies

I'D DARE TO MAKE MORE MISTAKES NEXT TIME.
I'D RELAX, I WOULD LIMBER UP. I WOULD BE SIL-
LIER THAN I HAVE BEEN THIS TRIP. I WOULD TAKE
FEWER THINGS SERIOUSLY. I WOULD TAKE MORE
CHANCES. I WOULD CLIMB MORE MOUNTAINS AND
SWIM MORE RIVERS. I WOULD PERHAPS HAVE
MORE ACTUAL TROUBLES, BUT I'D HAVE FEWER
IMAGINARY ONES.

YOU SEE, I'M ONE OF THOSE PEOPLE WHO LIVES
SENSIBLY AND SANELY HOUR AFTER HOUR, DAY
AFTER DAY. OH, I'VE HAD MY MOMENTS, AND IF
I HAD IT TO DO OVER AGAIN, I'D HAVE MORE OF
THEM. IN FACT, I'D TRY TO HAVE NOTHING ELSE.
JUST MOMENTS, ONE AFTER ANOTHER, INSTEAD
OF LIVING SO MANY YEARS AHEAD OF EACH DAY. I'VE
BEEN ONE OF THOSE PERSONS WHO NEVER GOES
ANYWHERE WITHOUT A THERMOMETER, A HOT
WATER BOTTLE, A RAINCOAT, AND A PARACHUTE.
IF I HAD TO DO IT AGAIN, I WOULD TRAVEL
LIGHTER THAN I HAVE.

IF I HAD MY LIFE TO LIVE OVER, I WOULD START
BAREFOOT EARLIER IN THE SPRING AND STAY THAT
WAY LATER IN THE FALL. I WOULD GO TO MORE
DANCES. I WOULD RIDE MORE MERRY-GO-ROUNDS.
I WOULD PICK MORE DAISIES.

—Nadine Stair, 85 years old, Louisville, Ky.
*(Reprinted from the Washington County [Ore.]
Mental Health Department newsletter.)*

*"Only in the part of us that we share,
can we understand each other."*
— *Anonymous*

WONDERFUL SUGAR COOKIES

(You will need additional time.)

1 cup butter or margarine	*1 1/4 cups rice flour*
1 1/2 cups granulated sugar	*1 cup bean flour*
or 1 cup honey	*1/2 teaspoon salt*
2 eggs	*1 teaspoon baking powder*
1 teaspoon vanilla extract	*3 teaspoons xanthan gum*

PREHEAT oven to 375°.

GREASE cookie sheet(s).

CREAM butter and sugar or honey.

ADD eggs and vanilla.

SIFT dry ingredients and ADD to butter mixture.

CHILL at least 1 hour.

ADD enough flour to make firm and ROLL out 1/8 inch thick.

CUT into desired shapes.

PLACE on greased cookie sheet(s).

BAKE at 375° for 8 minutes.

Yield: 30 cookies

CELEBRATION COOKIE

1 recipe Sugar Cookie dough
(see recipe on previous page)
1 5-ounce can vanilla pudding
1/3 cup peanut butter
1/4 cup plain yogurt

1 banana
Lemon juice
Jam or jelly, warmed
Dry roasted peanuts

PREHEAT oven to 400°.

GREASE cookie sheet.

ROLL dough into 8-inch circle.

PLACE on cookie sheet.

BAKE at 400° for 10 minutes or until browned.

COOL 5 minutes.

LOOSEN edges.

STIR together pudding and peanut butter.

GENTLY fold in yogurt.

SPREAD over crust.

SLICE banana diagonally and BRUSH with lemon juice.

LAYER slices on top of peanut butter mixture.

DRIZZLE warmed jam or jelly over slices.

SPRINKLE with dry roasted peanuts.

Husband Ed says these cookies are the best I make!

TOLL HOUSE COOKIES

1 cup shortening
1/2 cup granulated sugar
   (see note)
1 cup brown sugar (see note)
1 teaspoon vanilla extract
2 eggs, well-beaten
2/3 cup rice flour

2/3 cup bean flour
1 teaspoon baking soda
3/4 teaspoon salt
2 teaspoons xanthan gum
6 ounces chocolate chips
1 cup chopped nuts

PREHEAT oven to 300°.

GREASE cookie sheet(s).

CREAM shortening, sugars, and vanilla.

FOLD in eggs and BEAT mixture.

MIX in another bowl flours, baking soda, salt, and xanthan gum.

ADD to shortening mixture.

ADD chocolate chips and nuts.

DROP by teaspoonfuls 1/2 inch apart on cookie sheet(s).

BAKE at 300° for 15 minutes.

Note: You may substitute 1 cup honey for both sugars.

Yield: 100 cookies

CHEWY CHOCOLATE COOKIES

1 1/4 cups shortening
2 cups granulated sugar
2 eggs
2 teaspoons vanilla extract
1 cup bean flour
1 cup oat or rice flour

2 teaspoons xanthan gum
3/4 cup cocoa
1 teaspoon baking soda
1/2 teaspoon salt
1 cup chopped nuts

PREHEAT oven to 350°.

CREAM shortening and sugar.

ADD eggs and vanilla and BLEND.

COMBINE in another bowl flours, xanthan gum, cocoa, baking soda, and salt.

BLEND into shortening mixture.

STIR in nuts.

DROP by teaspoonfuls onto ungreased cookie sheet(s).

BAKE at 350° for 8 to 9 minutes. Do not overbake.

COOL 1 minute before removing from pan.

Yield: about 4 dozen

If you really *like brownies . . .*

A HONEY OF A BROWNIE MIX

4 1/2 cups rice flour
1 1/2 cups soy or bean flour
8 teaspoons baking powder
4 teaspoons salt

6 teaspoons xanthan gum
1 8-ounce can
   unsweetened cocoa

SIFT all ingredients together.

PUT into large airtight container and LABEL.

STORE in a cool dry place.

Yield: about 7 cups

A HONEY OF A BROWNIE

1 egg
1 teaspoon vanilla extract
2 cups Brownie Mix
   (see recipe above)

1 cup honey
1/2 cup canola oil
1/2 cup chopped nuts,
   divided

PREHEAT oven to 325°.

GREASE and FLOUR 8-inch square pan.

COMBINE egg, vanilla, honey, oil, and brownie mix.

BEAT until smooth.

STIR in nuts, reserving 1 to 2 tablespoons.

POUR into prepared pan.

SPRINKLE reserved nuts on top of batter.

BAKE at 325° for 35 minutes.

COOL. CUT into 2-inch square bars.

Oldest son Harvey doesn't like to be fooled!
"Are these wheat-free?" he asks. "You tell me!" answers Mom.

BROWNIES 2

2 squares unsweetened chocolate	1/8 teaspoon salt
or 6 tablespoons cocoa +	1/4 cup bean flour
2 tablespoons shortening	1 teaspoon xanthan gum
1/4 cup butter or margarine	1/4 cup rice flour
1 cup granulated sugar	1/2 cup chopped walnuts
2 eggs, unbeaten	1 teaspoon vanilla extract

PREHEAT oven to 325°.

GREASE 8 x 8 x 2-inch pan.

MIX chocolate and butter or margarine over hot water on low heat
or MICROWAVE 30 seconds.

REMOVE from heat.

STIR in remaining ingredients.

BAKE at 325° for 35 minutes until dry on top and almost firm.

COOL.

CUT into bars.

LEMON BARS

1 cup rice flour
1 cup bean flour
2 teaspoons xanthan gum
1 cup butter or margarine (see note)
About 4 cups lemon pie filling, canned
  or your own
1/2 cup powdered sugar (see note)

PREHEAT oven to 350°.

MIX flours, xanthan gum, and butter or margarine thoroughly.

PAT down in 9 x 13-inch baking dish.

BAKE at 350° for 15 to 25 minutes. COOL.

FILL with pie filling and SPRINKLE with powdered sugar

OR

FILL before baking shell.

BAKE at 350° for 25 minutes. COOL.

SPRINKLE with powdered sugar.

Note: If you use butter you can omit the sugar, but if you use margarine you must use the sugar.

ALMOND OATMEAL COOKIES

(You will need additional time.)

4 cups uncooked
  quick oatmeal
2 cups brown sugar
1 cup vegetable oil

2 eggs, beaten
1 teaspoon salt
1 teaspoon almond
  extract

PREHEAT oven to 325°.

GREASE cookie sheet(s).

MIX oatmeal, sugar, and oil and LET SET several hours
or overnight.

MIX in remaining ingredients.

DROP by teaspoonfuls onto greased cookie sheet(s).

BAKE at 325° for 15 minutes.

REMOVE cookies promptly to wire rack.

When I first visited my mother-in-law's home, she offered me . . .

ALMOND CAKES

(You will need additional time.)

8 ounces butter or margarine	*7/8 cup rice flour*
6 tablespoons granulated sugar	*7/8 cup bean flour*
1 teaspoon vanilla extract	*2 teaspoons xanthan gum*
2 ounces (1/2 cup) chopped almonds	*Powdered sugar*

PREHEAT oven to 300°.

GREASE cookie sheet(s).

CREAM butter, sugar, and vanilla.

ADD almonds, then flours and xanthan gum and MIX well.

REFRIGERATE 1 hour.

SHAPE in half-moons on greased cookie sheets.

BAKE at 300° for 25 minutes.

ROLL in powdered sugar or SHAKE in a bag of powdered sugar.

REMOVE from bag and COOL.

From Grandma Potts 1899-1995.

PEANUT BUTTER COOKIES

1/2 cup margarine or butter
1/2 cup peanut butter
1 cup packed brown sugar
1/2 teaspoon vanilla extract
3/4 cup bean flour

1/2 cup potato starch
1/2 teaspoon baking soda
1/2 teaspoon salt
1 teaspoon xanthan gum or
    1 egg (see note)

PREHEAT oven to 350°.

GREASE cookie sheet(s).

BEAT margarine or butter, peanut butter, sugar, and vanilla until creamy.

MIX in another bowl flours, baking soda, salt, and xanthan gum.

ADD to sugar mixture, and BEAT.

ROLL dough into 1-inch balls.

PLACE balls about 2 inches apart on greased cookie sheet(s).

PRESS balls with fork to make crisscross pattern.

BAKE at 350° for 15 minutes until slightly browned.

REMOVE cookies from pan and COOL.

Note: If you add 1 egg (to the butter mixture), you can omit xanthan gum.

Nut butters can be made in your food processor. Just process until smooth. Toasting nuts improves the flavor.

ALMOND BUTTER COOKIES

See note.
1 cup almond butter
1/2 cup honey
1/4 cup almond oil
1 teaspoon almond extract

1/4 teaspoon salt
2 cups arrowroot flour
1 teaspoon xanthan gum
  (optional)

PREHEAT oven to 350°.

GREASE cookie sheet(s).

COMBINE butter, honey, and oil and BLEND until smooth.

ADD almond extract and salt.

ADD flour a little at a time and MIX well.

FORM dough into balls and PLACE on greased cookie sheet.

FLATTEN balls with a fork to about 1/2-inch thickness.

BAKE at 350° for about 10 minutes.

Raw dough keeps well in the refrigerator for about 2 weeks.

Note: You can make many substitutions in this recipe. Experiment with different oils, nuts, and flours. Bean flour creates a totally different texture.

PEANUT BUTTER SQUARES

1 6-ounce package butterscotch or chocolate chips
1/2 cup peanut butter
3 cups Puffed Rice or Rice Krispies cereal

LINE cookie sheet with wax paper.

MELT chips and peanut butter over hot (not boiling) water.

REMOVE from heat, ADD cereal, and COMBINE.

DROP by tablespoonfuls onto wax paper.

REFRIGERATE until firm.

BOUNTY BARS

1/2 cup shortening
3/4 cup honey
2 eggs, slightly beaten
2 tablespoons milk or water
2 cups uncooked
   quick oatmeal

1 cup coconut
1 teaspoon almond extract
1/2 cup raisins
1/2 cup walnuts

PREHEAT oven to 350°.

GREASE 9 x 13-inch pan.

CREAM shortening and honey together.

BEAT in eggs and milk or water.

STIR in remaining ingredients.

PAT mixture into greased pan.

BAKE at 350° for 15 to 20 minutes.

MEXICAN WEDDING CAKES

(You will need additional time.)

1 cup butter or margarine
1/4 cup powdered sugar +
* additional (see note)*
1/8 teaspoon salt
2 teaspoons vanilla extract

7/8 cup rice flour
7/8 cup bean flour
2 teaspoons xanthan gum
1 cup chopped nuts

CREAM butter and 1/4 cup sugar.

ADD salt, vanilla, flours, xanthan gum, and nuts.

MIX to form dough.

COVER and CHILL dough 2 hours or overnight.

PREHEAT oven to 325°.

FORM dough into 1-inch balls.

PLACE on ungreased cookie sheet(s).

BAKE at 325° for 12 to 15 minutes.

REMOVE from oven and immediately ROLL in additional powdered sugar.

COOL. FREEZE if desired.

Yield: 48 cookies

Note: Substituting 1 cup granulated sugar totally changes the texture, making it very chewy and equally good.

A very chewy and filling cookie with lots of good-for-you ingredients.

OAT COOKIES

3/4 cup granulated sugar
1/3 cup margarine
1/3 cup honey
2 egg whites, slightly
beaten (see note)
1 teaspoon almond extract
2 1/4 cups uncooked
quick oats

1 cup oat flour
1/2 teaspoon baking soda
1/2 cup sliced almonds
1/2 teaspoon salt (optional)
1/3 cup raisins, chopped
prunes, or coconut
(optional)

PREHEAT oven to 350°.

BEAT in large bowl sugar, margarine, and honey until fluffy.

ADD egg whites and almond extract.

ADD dry ingredients and nuts gradually, MIXING well.

DROP by tablespoonfuls onto ungreased cookie sheet(s).

PRESS each into flattened circle.

BAKE at 350° for 14 to 16 minutes or until golden brown.

COOL for 1 minute and REMOVE from pan.

STORE in tightly covered tin.

Note: If you double the recipe, use 3 egg whites.

This is an easy recipe to make—no baking!
It also makes a good crumb crust for pies.

BOILED OATMEAL COOKIES

2 cups granulated sugar
4 tablespoons cocoa
1/2 cup margarine or butter
1/3 cup soy or rice milk
2 1/2 cups uncooked quick oats

1 teaspoon vanilla extract
1/3 cup peanut
  butter (optional)
1/4 cup chopped nuts

LINE a cookie sheet with wax paper.

MIX sugar, cocoa, margarine or butter, and soy or rice milk
in saucepan.

BRING mixture to rolling boil and BOIL for 2 minutes.

REMOVE from heat, ADD remaining ingredients, and MIX.

DROP warm batter by tablespoonfuls on wax paper. Mixture
becomes difficult to work with when it cools.

REMOVE cookies from wax paper when cool.

Yield: 24 to 30 cookies

As a little boy, oldest son Harvey really loved "spidercrotch."

OATMEAL SCOTCHIES

(as in butterscotch)
3/4 cup rice flour
3/4 cup bean flour
1 teaspoon baking soda
2 teaspoons baking powder
2 teaspoons xanthan gum
1 teaspoon salt
1 cup butter or margarine
1 1/2 cups packed
  brown sugar

2 eggs
1 tablespoon water
1 1/2 cups uncooked
  quick oats
1 12-ounce package
  butterscotch morsels
1/2 teaspoon orange extract

PREHEAT oven to 375°.

GREASE cookie sheets.

COMBINE flours, baking soda, baking powder, xanthan gum, and salt.

COMBINE in another bowl butter or margarine, sugar, eggs, and water.

BEAT until creamy.

ADD flour mixture gradually.

STIR in oats, butterscotch morsels, and orange extract.

DROP by tablespoonfuls onto greased cookie sheets.

BAKE at 375° for 10 to 12 minutes.

COOL slightly, then REMOVE cookies to wire rack.

Yield: 4 dozen

BLUEBERRY OAT BARS

1 3/4 cups uncooked
   quick oats
1 1/2 cups oat flour
1 1/2 teaspoons xanthan gum
3/4 cup packed brown
   sugar
1/2 cup chopped nuts
1/2 teaspoon baking soda
1/2 teaspoon salt (optional)

3/4 cup margarine,
   melted
2 cups fresh or frozen
   blueberries
1/2 cup granulated
   sugar
3 tablespoons water, divided
2 tablespoons cornstarch
2 teaspoons lemon juice

PREHEAT oven to 350°.

GREASE 12 x 9-inch glass baking dish.

COMBINE oats, flour, xanthan gum, brown sugar, nuts, baking soda, and salt, if using.

ADD margarine and MIX until crumbly.

RESERVE 3/4 cup mixture.

PRESS remaining mixture onto bottom of greased baking dish.

BAKE at 350° for 10 minutes.

COMBINE blueberries, granulated sugar, and 2 tablespoons water.

BRING to boil. SIMMER 2 minutes, uncovered, STIRRING occasionally.

COMBINE remaining 1 tablespoon water, cornstarch, and lemon juice.

STIR gradually into blueberry mixture.

COOK and STIR about 30 seconds or until thickened.

SPREAD over partially baked crust to within 1/4 inch of edge.

SPRINKLE with reserved oat mixture.

BAKE at 350° for 18 to 20 minutes or until topping is golden brown.

COOL in pan on wire rack.

CUT into bars.

STORE in tightly covered container.

PECAN PIE BARS

*1 cup + 1 tablespoon
  oat flour
1 teaspoon xanthan gum
1/2 cup uncooked quick
  oats
1/2 cup butter, softened
3/4 cup packed brown
  sugar*

*3 eggs
3/4 cup corn syrup
1 cupped chopped pecans
1/4 teaspoon salt
1 teaspoon vanilla extract*

PREHEAT oven to 350°.

GREASE 9-inch square pan.

COMBINE 1 cup flour, xanthan gum, oats, butter, and sugar.

PRESS into bottom of pan.

BAKE at 350° for 15 minutes.

BEAT eggs, corn syrup, pecans, vanilla, salt, and 1 tablespoon flour.

POUR over baked crust.

BAKE at 350° for 25 to 30 minutes.

COOL in pan on wire rack.

CUT into bars while still slightly warm.

One of my favorites . . .

MAPLE BARS

1 cup unsalted butter	*2/3 cup oat flour*
1 cup granulated sugar or	*1 1/2 teaspoons xanthan gum*
2/3 cup honey	*4 teaspoons baking powder*
2 teaspoons vanilla extract	*2 cups uncooked quick oats*
2 teaspoons maple extract	*1 cup finely chopped walnuts*
2 large eggs	*1 cup flaked coconut*
2/3 cup rice flour	

PREHEAT oven to 300°.

BUTTER 9 x 13-inch baking pan.

BEAT together butter, sugar or honey, extracts, and eggs in large bowl.

SIFT into another bowl flours, xanthan gum, and baking powder.

STIR into liquid mixture.

BLEND in oats, walnuts, and coconut.

SPREAD batter evenly in buttered pan.

BAKE at 300° for 50 minutes, until lightly browned.

COOL and CUT into bars.

SCOTCH SHORTBREAD

1/2 pound butter
1/4 cup granulated sugar
1 cup bean flour

2 cups rice flour
3 teaspoons xanthan gum

PREHEAT oven to 300°.

CREAM butter and sugar. ADD flours and xanthan gum.

PRESS into ungreased 8-inch square pan.

BAKE at 300° for 1 hour. COOL and CUT into squares.

RUSSIAN TEACAKES

1 cup butter or margarine
1 cup + additional
  powdered sugar
1 teaspoon salt
1 teaspoon vanilla extract

2 cups rice flour
2 teaspoons xanthan gum
1 cup finely chopped
  hazelnuts or pecans

PREHEAT oven to 325°.

CREAM butter and sugar in large bowl.

ADD salt and vanilla and MIX well.

STIR in flour, xanthan gum, and nuts.

DIVIDE dough into 1-inch balls and PLACE 1 1/2 inches apart on
ungreased cookie sheet(s).

BAKE at 325° for 10 minutes.

ROLL in powdered sugar immediately, then COOL on wire rack.

ROLL again in powdered sugar. Rolling twice is important.

Ed's favorite cookies as a child.
Grandma Potts made them for her children.

BUTTERSCOTCH ICE BOX COOKIES

(You will need additional time.)

1/2 cup butter or margarine
1 cup dark brown sugar
1 egg, slightly beaten
1/2 teaspoon vanilla extract
3/4 cup rice flour
3/4 cup bean flour

1 1/2 teaspoons xanthan gum
1/2 teaspoon cream of tartar
1/2 teaspoon baking soda
1/2 cup ground walnuts or
  any other nuts

PREHEAT oven to 375°.

GREASE cookie sheet(s).

CREAM butter and sugar in large bowl.

ADD egg and vanilla and MIX well.

MIX in another bowl flours, xanthan gum, cream of tartar, and baking soda.

ADD to butter mixture. ADD nuts.

FORM dough into roll and WRAP in wax paper or plastic wrap.

REFRIGERATE at least 2 hours.

SLICE roll into 1/4-inch cookies.

PLACE on greased cookie sheet(s).

BAKE at 375° for 8 minutes or until lightly browned.

Good served with fruit.

ANISE COOKIES

2 eggs	*1 teaspoon xanthan gum*
2/3 cup granulated sugar	*1/2 cup rice flour*
1 teaspoon anise seed	*1/2 cup bean or millet flour*

PREHEAT oven to 350°.

GREASE and FLOUR loaf pan (about 9 x 5 x 3-inches).

BEAT eggs and sugar in medium bowl.

ADD anise seed, then flours and xanthan gum.

SPREAD batter in prepared pan (pan will only be 1/4 full).

BAKE at 350° for 30 minutes.

BUTTER cookie sheets.

REMOVE loaf from pan and slice in 1/2-inch slices.

PLACE slices on buttered cookie sheet and BAKE at 350° for 5 minutes.

TURN slices and BAKE 5 more minutes or until sides are browned.

COOL.

Sometimes coconut is packaged with preservatives to sweeten it and keep it soft. If you are sensitive to such things, read the label.

COCONUT COOKIES

3 eggs
1/2 cup honey
2 tablespoons oil
2 cups shredded dry
  coconut (see note)

1 1/2 cups oat flour
  (see note)
2 teaspoons baking powder
1 teaspoon xanthan gum
Candied cherries

PREHEAT oven to 325°.

GREASE cookie sheets.

BEAT together eggs, honey, and oil in large bowl.

ADD coconut.

MIX in another bowl flour, baking powder, and xanthan gum.

ADD to coconut mixture and MIX thoroughly.

DROP by teaspoonfuls on greased cookie sheets.

FLATTEN lightly and TOP with 1/2 candied cherry.

BAKE at 325° for 10 minutes.

Yield: 4 dozen

Note: This recipe uses dry coconut. If you substitute moistened, reduce liquid by 1 1/2 teaspoons for each 1/2 cup dry coconut.

COCONUT MACAROONS

1/4 cup rice flour
1/4 cup bean flour
1/2 teaspoon salt
2/3 cup milk or water
14 ounces flaked dry
   coconut

3 tablespoons corn syrup
1 1/2 teaspoons vanilla
   extract
1/2 teaspoon almond
   extract

PREHEAT oven to 325°. GREASE and FLOUR cookie sheets.

MIX dry ingredients. ADD remaining ingredients and MIX.

DROP by tablespoonfuls onto cookie sheets.

BAKE at 325° for 20 minutes.

Yield: 4 dozen

CHOCOLATE MARSHMALLOW COOKIES

1 cup Puffed Rice cereal
1 cup chocolate chips
1 1/2 cups small marshmallows

1 cup dry coconut
1/2 cup chopped walnuts

PREHEAT oven to 350°.

GREASE 8 x 8 x 2-inch baking dish.

COVER bottom of dish with cereal.

TOP with chocolate chips, then marshmallows, then coconut.

POUR nuts over all.

BAKE at 350° for 20 minutes.

TOFU BARS

4 tablespoons butter
  or margarine
1/2 cup honey
1 teaspoon vanilla extract
1/4 teaspoon salt
1/3 cup tofu

1/2 cup rice flour
1/2 teaspoon xanthan gum
1 teaspoon baking soda
1 teaspoon baking powder
1/2 cup chopped nuts

PREHEAT oven to 325°.

GREASE 8 x 8 x 2-inch pan.

MELT butter and stir in honey.

COMBINE with remaining ingredients except nuts in processor
or blender.

MIX until well blended.

POUR into pan.

SPRINKLE nuts on top.

BAKE at 325° for 40 minutes. COOL.

CUT into bars.

SUPERMOUSE BARS

1/4 cup honey
2 tablespoons oil
3 tablespoons
  peanut butter
3/4 cup oat or rice bran
3/4 cup uncooked
  quick oats

1/2 cup unsweetened
  coconut
1/2 cup finely chopped
  dried apricots

GREASE 8 x 8-inch pan.

MELT honey, oil, and peanut butter together in large saucepan at medium heat.

ADD remaining ingredients and MIX well.

STIR 5 minutes and REMOVE from heat.

PRESS mixture evenly into pan.

REFRIGERATE until firm and CUT into bars.

*If you must avoid eggs, you'll like these very crisp cookies—
and they're great for dunking.*

GINGERSNAPS

(You will need additional time.)

1 cup molasses
1/2 cup granulated sugar
3 tablespoons butter or
  margarine
3 tablespoons lard
2 tablespoons water
1 1/2 cups rice flour

1 1/2 cups bean flour
3 teaspoons xanthan gum
1 teaspoon baking soda
1 teaspoon cloves
1 teaspoon cinnamon
1 teaspoon ginger
1 teaspoon salt

PREHEAT oven to 325°.

BRING molasses to a boil in saucepan.

ADD sugar, butter or margarine, lard, and water.

COMBINE dry ingredients in large bowl and ADD to sugar mixture.

CHILL overnight.

ROLL dough to about 1/8-inch thick and CUT into rounds or
gingerbread men (see note).

PLACE on ungreased cookie sheet.

BAKE at 325° about 10 minutes.

Note: You can also form dough into a log shape, refrigerate up to
2 weeks, then make 1/8-inch slices.

Yield: about 10 dozen

Very crisp cookies were prized in days gone by because they kept a
long time. They will soften if you add a little piece of apple to the
cookie tin.

Another cookie without eggs, this recipe is adapted from
Pennsylvania Dutch Cookery *by Ann Hark and Preston Barba*
(no longer in print).

EGGLESS MOLASSES COOKIES

(You will need additional time.)

2 cups brown sugar
1 cup shortening
1 cup molasses
1/2 cup warm water
1 teaspoon baking soda

2 1/2 cups rice flour
2 cups bean flour
4 teaspoons xanthan gum
1 teaspoon cinnamon

CREAM sugar and shortening.

ADD molasses.

DISSOLVE baking soda in water.

COMBINE in another bowl flours, xanthan gum, and cinnamon.

ADD flours and water alternately to molasses mixture.

MIX well.

SHAPE dough into a long roll, about 2 1/2 inches in diameter.

FLATTEN slightly and REFRIGERATE overnight.

PREHEAT oven to 350°.

CUT roll into 1/4-inch slices.

PLACE on ungreased cookie sheet(s).

BAKE at 350° for about 12 minutes.

Yield: 50 cookies

Lebkuchen is a Pennsylvania Dutch specialty and a wonderful cookie with the added bonus of not needing eggs. These keep very well in a tightly closed cookie tin.

LEBKUCHEN

(You will need additional time.)

1 1/2 cups honey
2 1/4 cups brown sugar
1/2 cup butter or margarine
3 cups rice flour
2 1/2 cups bean flour
1/2 teaspoon salt
5 teaspoons xanthan gum
1/2 teaspoon cloves
1/2 teaspoon mace
1/2 teaspoon cardamom
1 teaspoon cinnamon
3/4 cup chopped citron
1 1/4 cups chopped almonds

Glaze:
 2 tablespoons water
 1 cup powdered sugar
 1 teaspoon lemon juice
 3/4 cup chopped citron
 1 1/4 cups chopped
  almonds

HEAT honey, sugar, and butter or margarine.

COMBINE in another bowl flours, salt, xanthan gum, cloves, mace, cardamom, and cinnamon.

ADD to honey mixture and STIR.

ADD citron and nuts.

KNEAD dough and PLACE in covered bowl.

SET ASIDE for a week in a cool place.

PREHEAT oven to 325°. GREASE cookie sheets.

ROLL dough 1/4 inch thick (Takes a bit of elbow grease!).

PLACE on greased cookie sheets, or press into cookie tin with a rim around it.

BAKE at 325° about 15 minutes until dark brown.

COMBINE glaze ingredients.

REMOVE Lebkuchen from oven and BRUSH with glaze.

CUT into squares while still warm.

Caroline Schnoor, of Portland, Ore., explains that Christmas baking used to start way before Christmas, so cookies were very hard in order to preserve them. They would be softened by Christmas, or a piece of apple would be put in the cookie tin for a day or two. My friend Carol Groff from Canby, Ore., treats her family to glazed Lebkuchen.

A Moravian (German) Christmas cake—another wonderful eggless cookie! In the old days these were also made hard in order to preserve them.

LECKERLE

(You will need additional time.)

1 1/2 teaspoons baking soda	1/3 cup diced citron
1 tablespoon warm water	1/4 cup chopped,
2 cups molasses	blanched almonds
1/4 cup melted butter	2 cups rice flour
or margarine	2 cups bean flour
1 cup brown sugar	4 teaspoons xanthan gum
1 1/2 teaspoons cloves	1 ounce (2 tablespoons)
1 tablespoon cinnamon	brandy

DISSOLVE baking soda in water and SET ASIDE.

HEAT molasses in a large saucepan.

ADD butter or margarine, sugar, cloves, cinnamon, citron, nuts, and baking soda solution.

COMBINE flours and xanthan gum and ADD to molasses mixture a little at a time.

ADD brandy a little at a time.

COVER dough and SET ASIDE in a cool place 2 weeks.

PREHEAT oven to 325°.

GREASE cookie sheets.

ROLL dough 1/4 inch thick on lightly floured board (with vigor!).

CUT into 4-inch squares.

PLACE on greased cookie sheets.

BAKE at 325° for about 15 minutes.

These cakes will keep about 2 months in a tightly closed cookie tin.

*These Pennsylvania Dutch cookies are unique in that
a mold is pressed upon the rolled-out dough.*

SPRINGERLE

(You will need additional time.)

2 eggs
1 cup granulated sugar
1 lemon rind, grated
*2 teaspoons aniseed or
  few drops anise oil*
*3/4 cup + additional
  rice flour*

3/4 cup bean flour
1 1/2 teaspoons xanthan gum
*1 teaspoon baking powder or
  baking soda*
1/4 teaspoon salt

BEAT eggs lightly. ADD sugar slowly and BEAT 15 minutes.

ADD lemon rind.

ADD remaining ingredients. If dough is still rather soft, KNEAD in
a little more rice flour.

ROLL 1/4 inch thick and as close as possible to shape of Springerle
mold (see note).

FLOUR surface of dough and PRESS mold into dough.

CUT into little squares (a pizza cutter works well).

PLACE on greased and floured cookie sheets.

COVER lightly with cloths and refrigerate 24 hours to dry and to set
impressions in dough.

(In the old days cookies were left on the kitchen counter to cure.

Now, because we use eggs, we refrigerate them.)

BAKE at 300° for 25 minutes. Do not brown. Cookies will be very
crisp. A piece of apple in the cookie tin for a day or two will soften
them.

Note: Springerle molds are found in kitchen stores.

How long has it been since you've had an ice cream cone?

ICE CREAM CONES

3 eggs (see note)
1/2 cup rice flour
1/4 cup arrowroot flour
1/4 cup bean flour

1 teaspoon xanthan gum
1 cup granulated sugar
1 tablespoon or more water

PREHEAT oven to 350°.

GREASE cookie sheet.

WHIP eggs, flours, xanthan gum, and sugar.

ADD water, more if dough is too thick to spread. (It should feel like you are spreading bubble gum.)

PLACE spoonfuls of batter about the size of ping-pong balls on greased cookie sheet.

DIP a spatula in cold water and SMOOTH each ball into a thin oval pancake.

BAKE at 350° about 10 minutes, until just barely browned.

Immediately REMOVE pancakes and ROLL into cones before they become too crisp. (I use a rubber glove on my left hand to keep from burning my fingers and a spatula in my right hand to loosen the pancakes.)

STORE in airtight tin for later use.

Warning: These are good enough to disappear before you even fill your cookie tin!

Note: I have used Ener-g Foods Egg Replacer, found at your health food store. You may have to experiment a little.

Sweets

*THERE ARE IN THE END,
THREE THINGS THAT LAST:
FAITH, HOPE, AND LOVE,
AND THE GREATEST OF
THESE IS LOVE.*

—I Corinthians 13:13

*OH, MY FRIENDS, BE WARNED BY ME,
THAT BREAKFAST, DINNER, LUNCH AND TEA
ARE ALL THE HUMAN FRAME REQUIRES . . .*

—Hilaire Belloc

Paul Kyllo, a great taster of experimental recipes,
gave me this recipe.

SWEET COCONUT RICE

1/2 cup coconut milk (see note)
1/2 cup water
2 cups cooked rice (any type)

BRING coconut milk and water to boil in top of double boiler.

ADD rice, STIRRING only to keep it from sticking to pan.

PLACE pan on direct heat.

COVER and SIMMER 12 minutes.

REMOVE from heat, COVER and LET STAND 10 minutes.

Tastes great warm or cold, with milk, nuts, raisins, etc.

Note: Or use soy milk plus 1/4 cup flaked coconut.

This is a good dessert and a great way to use leftover breads, even some of your not-so-successful ones!

STEAMED BREAD PUDDING

1/2 cup brown sugar	1/4 cup butter, softened
1/2 cup raisins	2 cups soy milk or water
3 to 4 slices bread,	1 teaspoon vanilla extract
buttered on one side	1/2 teaspoon cinnamon
3 eggs	1/4 teaspoon salt

MIX sugar and raisins in oiled top of double boiler.

CUT buttered bread into 1/2-inch cubes.

PLACE cubes on top of sugar mixture.

BEAT eggs lightly in medium bowl.

ADD remaining ingredients to eggs. Don't overmix.

POUR egg mixture over bread cubes.

COOK over simmering water about 1 1/2 hours

OR

BAKE at 350° for 1 1/4 hours, until a knife inserted in center comes out fairly clean.

Friend Steve Sinner says these were good the day he installed our heating system, but were better served cold the day after!

PEACH DUMPLINGS

*1 tablespoon butter or
  margarine
1 cup granulated sugar
1 cup hot water
2 cups sliced peaches
1/2 cup rice flour*

*1/2 cup bean flour
1 teaspoon xanthan gum
2 teaspoons baking powder
1/2 teaspoon cinnamon
Dash salt
3/4 cup cold water*

COMBINE butter, sugar, and hot water in large saucepan.

BRING to boil and COOK until syrup forms.

ADD peaches and BRING to boil.

COMBINE dry ingredients in another bowl and ADD water.

DROP mixture by spoonfuls into boiling peach mixture.

COOK uncovered 10 minutes.

COVER and SIMMER 20 minutes. SERVE hot.

STRAWBERRY NONCAKE

SPOON a sauce of strawberries and a little sugar over canned pear half.

ADD nuts and whipped topping.

BLACKBERRY MUSH

1/3 cup water
4 cups blackberries, washed (see note)
3/4 cup granulated sugar
3 tablespoons cornstarch or tapioca
1/2 teaspoon vanilla extract

ADD water to berries and BOIL until berries are soft.

MASH berries and PUT through strainer.

ADD sugar and cornstarch or tapioca.

BOIL until thick, STIRRING constantly.

REMOVE from heat, ADD vanilla, and CHILL.

Note: You may substitute other berries or fruits.

The way Great Grandmother did it . . .

QUINCE APPLESAUCE

1/4 bushel apples
1 or 2 quinces
Honey

PREPARE apples for sauce.

COOK in large saucepan.

ADD quinces.

ADD honey to taste after cooking.

CHEESE-FILLED PEARS

2 large or 4 small pears
1 cup (6 ounces) Stilton or feta cheese
1/2 cup chopped walnuts

WASH pears, CUT in half, and CORE.

CRUMBLE cheese and MIX with walnuts.

PILE into pear halves.

THE FLAVOR OF VANILLA

A vanilla pod makes a wonderful flavoring. Steeped in milk for hot chocolate, it creates a marvelous drink, as does steeping it in wine. Steep the pod in the boiling liquid 10 to 15 minutes. When you have the flavor to your liking, rinse the pod in cold water and keep it in an airtight container. It should keep about 4 months. Keeping a piece of the pod in a sugar canister will flavor the sugar nicely. Then use to flavor a pudding or sauce.

For a quick, creamy dessert . . .

VANILLA PUDDING

6 tablespoons arrowroot flour	1/2 cup maple syrup
4 cups soy or rice milk, divided	Pinch salt
	2 teaspoons vanilla extract
	1/2 teaspoon nutmeg

DISSOLVE arrowroot in 1/4 cup milk and SET ASIDE.

COMBINE remaining milk, maple syrup, and salt in large saucepan.

BRING to boil over medium heat, STIRRING constantly.

ADD arrowroot mixture and STIR until mixture thickens.

REMOVE from heat.

STIR in vanilla and nutmeg.

POUR into serving dishes and REFRIGERATE until serving.

CHOCOLATE PUDDING MIX

1 1/2 cups + 2 tablespoons unsweetened cocoa powder
3 1/4 cups granulated sugar
1 1/2 cups cornstarch
1/2 teaspoon salt

MIX all ingredients well.

PLACE in a labeled container with tight-fitting lid.

STORE in a cool, dry place, 2 to 3 months.

NOW FOR SOME CHOCOLATE PUDDING!

(You will need additional time.)
  2 3/4 cups soy or rice milk
  2/3 cup Chocolate Pudding
    Mix (see recipe on previous page)
  2 tablespoons butter or margarine
  1 teaspoon vanilla extract

COMBINE milk and pudding mix in medium saucepan.

COOK and STIR over medium heat until mixture thickens.

COOK 1 minute longer.

REMOVE from heat and STIR in butter or margarine and vanilla.

POUR pudding into 6 custard cups.

COVER each with plastic wrap.

REFRIGERATE at least 1 hour.

Yield: 6 servings

If you are in the mood for some quick, safe ice cream, try this . . .

FROZEN DELIGHTS

(You will need additional time.)

PREPARE vanilla or chocolate pudding (see recipes above).

COOL completely.

SPOON into popsicle-type molds.

FREEZE overnight.

Use different fruits and flavorings in this recipe.

APPLE TAPIOCA

4 cups sliced apples
1/2 cup quick-cooking
  tapioca
1/2 teaspoon salt
1/2 to 1 cup brown or
  granulated sugar

2 teaspoons lemon juice
3 cups water
Cinnamon
Cloves
Allspice

PREHEAT oven to 325°.

GREASE 9 x 14-inch baking dish.

PLACE fruit in dish. SET ASIDE.

COMBINE tapioca, salt, sugar, and lemon juice.

ADD water and MIX.

BRING to boil over medium heat, STIRRING constantly.

POUR over fruit.

SPRINKLE spices over fruit.

COVER and BAKE at 325° about 45 minutes.

Yield: 6 servings

As close as you can come to wheat- and dairy-free ice cream . . .

PEAR SORBET WITH PEAR BRANDY

(You will need additional time.)
   2 pounds fresh ripe pears (Bartletts are excellent)
   1 teaspoon fresh lemon or lime juice
   2 tablespoons pear brandy

PEEL, CORE, and STEM pears.

PUREE pears with lemon juice.

TRANSFER to ice cream freezer.

CHURN until mixture becomes slushy.

ADD pear brandy and CHURN to combine.

TASTE!

PLACE in container just large enough to hold sorbet and
COVER tightly.

FREEZE several hours.

LET SOFTEN slightly before serving.

Matt Kramer provided this recipe.

BOYSENBERRY SORBET

3 cups boysenberries
1 cup honey
2 egg whites (optional)

1 1/3 cups water
2 tablespoons
 lemon juice

PUT berries, honey, water, and lemon juice into processor.

PROCESS until well mixed.

STRAIN to remove seeds if desired.

BEAT egg whites in separate bowl.

FOLD into berry mixture.

COOL, then POUR into ice cream freezer bucket.

FOLLOW directions for your ice cream maker.

CRAN-RASPBERRY SORBET

1/4 cup water
1/4 cup granulated sugar
3 1/4 cups cranberry-raspberry juice, chilled

SIMMER water and sugar in saucepan over low heat until sugar is dissolved.

COOL to room temperature.

ADD cranberry-raspberry juice.

FREEZE in bowl of ice cream machine according to maker's instructions.

Yield: 5 cups or 10 servings

Librarian Valerie McQuaid made this recipe for her daughter,
Kerry. Play with it by adding fruit or fruit syrups.

ALMOST ICE CREAM

4 eggs
2 cups rice or soy milk
1 teaspoon vanilla extract
  (see note)

1/2 cup honey
1/2 cup corn oil

BEAT all ingredients together.

FREEZE in a quart container.

Note: You can also flavor the ice cream by omitting vanilla extract and soaking a piece of vanilla bean in the milk overnight. Then remove the bean and save for another day.

One of Dr. John Green's favorites . . .

MAPLE TOPPED POPCORN

2 cups maple syrup
Oil or butter
10 to 12 cups popcorn

ADD a little oil or butter to maple syrup.

COOK to soft ball stage or harder for popcorn balls.

POUR warm topping over popcorn and SHAPE popcorn into balls. Yummy!

Also, great over Rice Dream (a diary-free "ice cream" health food stores and some supermarkets carry) or gingerbread.

BLUEBERRY RHUBARB CONSERVE

(You will need additional time.)

3 cups rhubarb in
1-inch pieces
3 cups fresh or frozen
blueberries

5 cups granulated sugar
Juice of 1/2 lemon
2 small packages (6 ounces)
raspberry gelatin

MIX rhubarb, blueberries, sugar, and lemon juice and LET STAND overnight in refrigerator.

BRING mixture to boil in large saucepan over low heat and COOK 12 minutes.

REMOVE from heat and STIR in gelatin.

POUR into hot sterilized jars and SEAL with paraffin.

I can hear my mother, Rose, saying, "Waste not, want not!"
The Honnold family never did!

APPLE JELLY

Peelings from 6 to 7 apples
2 cups water
Pinch cream of tartar
1 tablespoon powdered pectin
or 1 tablespoon vinegar

1 1/3 cups granulated sugar
Pinch of salt

BOIL peelings in water 20 minutes.

STRAIN off juice and MEASURE 1 1/2 cups into large saucepan.

ADD cream of tartar.

SIMMER 5 minutes.

ADD pectin or vinegar.

ADD sugar and salt.

FAST BOIL 7 minutes.

POUR into hot sterilized glasses and SEAL with paraffin.

Making your own syrup protects you from hidden wheat and preservatives.

RASPBERRY SYRUP

> 1 10-ounce package frozen raspberries or strawberries
> 2 cups granulated sugar
> 1/2 cup water

COMBINE all ingredients in medium saucepan.

BRING to boil and CONTINUE boiling until sugar melts.

SKIM off foam.

POUR into hot sterilized jars and SEAL.

Yield: 2 cups

GRAPE SYRUP

> 1 cup grape juice
> 2 cups granulated sugar
> 1 tablespoon lemon juice

COMBINE grape juice and sugar in medium saucepan.

BRING to boil.

SKIM off foam.

ADD lemon juice.

POUR into hot sterilized jars and SEAL.

Yield: 2 cups

APPLE SYRUP

1 cup apple juice
2 cups granulated sugar
Cinnamon stick

COMBINE all ingredients in medium saucepan.

BRING to boil.

SKIM off foam.

POUR into hot sterilized jars and SEAL.

Yield: 2 cups

ORANGE SYRUP

1 cup orange juice
2 cups granulated sugar
2 tablespoons lemon juice

COMBINE orange juice and sugar in medium saucepan.

BRING to boil.

SKIM off foam.

ADD lemon juice.

POUR into hot sterilized jars and SEAL.

Yield: 2 cups

CHOCOLATE SYRUP

1/4 cup corn syrup
1/2 cup granulated sugar
1/2 cup water

1 square (1 ounce)
    unsweetened chocolate
1/2 teaspoon vanilla extract

COOK corn syrup, sugar, and water in medium saucepan until mixture forms a soft ball when dropped into cold water.

REMOVE from heat and ADD chocolate and vanilla.

THIN (if needed) by adding cream.

STORE in jar in the refrigerator.

The only rationalization I can come up with for making candy is that at least you know what goes into it—no hidden wheat or malt or preservatives. It makes a wonderful treat.

EASY MINTS

3 egg whites
6 cups powdered sugar

Food coloring
Mint extract

BEAT egg whites until stiff.

BLEND in sugar.

TINT with food coloring and FLAVOR with mint extract.

ROLL out between sheets of wax paper.

CUT patties.

LET dry overnight on the counter.

ROCKY ROAD CANDY

1 12-ounce package semisweet chocolate morsels
2 tablespoons butter or margarine
2 cups nuts
1 10 1/2-ounce package minimarshmallows

MELT morsels in glass bowl in microwave or over a double boiler.

STIR in remaining ingredients.

DROP by tablespoonfuls onto wax paper

OR

SPREAD in wax paper-lined 13 x 9-inch pan.

CHILL until firm, about 2 hours.

We sold this caramel corn every year as a 4-H fundraiser
at the Clackamas County (Ore.) Fairgrounds . . .

CARAMEL CORN

2 cups brown sugar
1 cup margarine
1/2 cup corn syrup
1 teaspoon vanilla extract
1/2 teaspoon baking soda

10 to 12 cups popped
  popcorn
Whole pecans and almonds
  (optional)

MICROWAVE sugar, margarine, and corn syrup in a medium bowl
on high 4 minutes, STIRRING after 2 minutes
OR
BOIL 5 minutes, then BAKE at 250° for 1 hour, STIRRING every
15 minutes.
ADD vanilla and baking soda and MIX WELL.
ADD mixture to popcorn.
ADD pecans and almonds, if using.
FILL brown bag with 1/2 popcorn mixture.
FOLD bag and MICROWAVE on high 1 1/2 minutes.
TAKE out bag and SHAKE.
MICROWAVE bag for another 1 1/2 minutes.
SHAKE bag again.
SPREAD out to cool.

When Bob Myers comes for Thanksgiving,
he gets very excited about these . . .

PRALINES

2 cups granulated sugar
1 cup packed brown sugar
8 tablespoons (1 cube)
  unsalted butter

1 cup milk
2 teaspoons corn syrup
4 cups pecan halves
  (or equivalent pieces)

COMBINE all ingredients except pecans in medium saucepan.

BRING to boil.

COOK over low heat 20 minutes.

STIR in pecans and COOK until mixture forms a soft ball when dropped into cold water.

STIR well and DROP by tablespoonfuls onto wax paper.

COOL and WRAP individually with wax paper.

Yield: 2 1/2 dozen

NUT CLUSTERS

(You will need additional time.)
  1/2 pound Spanish peanuts, almonds, or dry cereal
  7 to 8 ounces (2 cups) semisweet chocolate chips

MELT chocolate in top of double boiler.

REMOVE from heat.

ADD nuts and STIR.

DROP by teaspoonfuls onto wax paper.

CHILL 12 hours.

SKILLET TOFFEE

3 cups granulated sugar
1 pound butter
1/2 cup chopped walnuts
1 cup chocolate chips

GREASE 9 x 12-inch pan.

COOK all ingredients except chocolate chips until candy thermometer registers 310°.

POUR into greased pan.

ADD chocolate chips on top, SPREADING with a knife as they melt.

CUT into pieces.

Make this fudge on the stove or in the microwave.

CAROL'S FUDGE

1 package chocolate chips	2 cups granulated sugar
or 1 cup peanut butter	1 12-ounce can evaporated milk
1 teaspoon vanilla extract	10 (7 ounces) marshmallows
6 tablespoons butter	Nuts (optional)

Stovetop Method:

BUTTER 9 x 13-inch pan.

COMBINE chips or peanut butter, vanilla, and butter in large bowl.

PUT sugar, milk, and marshmallows in large heavy saucepan.

HEAT sugar mixture to a rolling boil, then COOK 5 minutes only, STIRRING with wooden spoon.

POUR over chocolate chip or peanut butter mixture.

ADD nuts, if using, BEAT, and SPOON into buttered pan.

Microwave Method:

BUTTER 9 x 13-inch pan.

MICROWAVE butter in 4-quart bowl on high 1 minute or until melted.

ADD sugar and milk and MICROWAVE 5 minutes or until mix comes to a rolling boil.

STIR after 3 minutes and MIX well.

MICROWAVE 5 1/2 more minutes, STIRRING after 3 minutes.

STIR in chocolate chips or peanut butter, vanilla, and marshmallows.

BLEND well. POUR into buttered pan.

COOL before cutting.

Yield: 3 pounds

VERY LIKE APPLETS

(You will need additional time.)

2 tablespoons plain gelatin

1 1/4 cups warm applesauce, divided (see note)

2 cups raw or brown sugar

1 cup walnuts or almonds

1 teaspoon vanilla

Powdered sugar

GREASE 8 x 8-inch pan.

DISSOLVE gelatin in 1/2 cup warm applesauce and SET ASIDE.

COMBINE remaining applesauce with sugar in large saucepan.

BOIL 10 minutes.

ADD gelatin mixture and BOIL 15 minutes, STIRRING constantly.

REMOVE from heat and ADD nuts and vanilla.

POUR into greased pan.

LET stand overnight.

CUT into squares and DUST with powdered sugar.

Yum-m-m-m.

Note: Use a thick apricot or grape puree for two tasty variations.

*In addition to his wonderful wood creations, craftsman
extraordinaire Jim Knull makes these old fashioned . . .*

HOREHOUND DROPS

(You will need additional time.)
    6 tablespoons horehound leaves and stems
    1 1/2 cups boiling water
    3 1/2 cups brown sugar

CRUSH herbs and PLACE in teapot.

COVER with boiling water and STEEP 30 minutes.

STRAIN and POUR liquid over sugar.

MIX in large saucepan and BRING to a boil.

BOIL until mixture reaches the hard crack stage (separates into
threads when dropped into cold water): 300° on candy thermometer.

POUR into buttered 9 x 13 x 1-pan and CUT into squares.

These are very good for coughs and sore throats!

Enid France of Alexandria, Va., shares this sinful recipe with us.

NUTTY CHOCOLATE TRUFFLES

(You will need additional time.)

1/4 cup light cream (see note)
6 ounces semisweet baking
  chocolate
2 tablespoons grain-free
  orange- or raspberry-
  flavored liqueur or
  dark rum (optional)

1/4 cup butter, softened
  (see note)
1/2 cup coarsely chopped,
  toasted walnuts
Powdered sugar (see note)

BRING cream to boil in small saucepan.

BOIL 2 minutes or until reduced by half. REMOVE from heat.

BREAK up chocolate and ADD.

STIR until chocolate melts. ADD liqueur, if using.

STIR in butter and nuts and MIX well.

SPOON mixture into soup-size bowl.

REFRIGERATE until firm, about 1 hour.

FILL a custard cup about halfway with sugar.

SCOOP chilled chocolate with teaspoon and ROLL between hands
to shape into 1-inch balls. (This will be messy!)

DROP balls into sugar and TOSS to coat.

PLACE truffles in individual candy cups.

STORE in covered container in refrigerator.

BRING truffles to room temperature 15 minutes before serving.

Note: I have substituted rice milk and margarine with success. If you
must avoid corn, omit powdered sugar because it contains cornstarch;
try substituting cocoa.

Cereals

I SEE NO HOPE FOR THE FUTURE OF OUR PEOPLE IF THEY ARE DEPENDENT ON THE FRIVOLOUS YOUTH OF TODAY FOR CERTAINLY ALL YOUTH ARE RECKLESS BEYOND WORDS . . . WHEN I WAS A BOY WE WERE TAUGHT TO BE DISCREET AND RESPECTFUL OF OUR ELDERS, BUT THE PRESENT YOUTH ARE EXCEEDINGLY WISE AND IMPATIENT OF ALL RESTRAINT.

—Hesiod, 8th century B.C.

SPARE YOUR BREATH TO COOL YOUR PORRIDGE.

—Rabelais

It thrills me to know my friend Linda from Vanuatu (formerly New Hebrides) still uses my recipe for granola after 25 years!

GRANOLA

6 cups quick oats, uncooked
1/2 cup firmly packed
   brown sugar (see note)
3/4 cup oat bran
1/2 cup flaked or
   shredded coconut
1/2 cup sunflower seeds,
   raw or roasted

1/3 cup sesame seeds
1 cup chopped nuts
1/2 cup vegetable oil
1/3 cup honey (see note)
1 1/2 teaspoons vanilla or
   almond extract

HEAT oats in large roasting pan at 350° for 10 minutes.

COMBINE oats, sugar, bran, coconut, seeds, and nuts.

ADD oil, honey, and vanilla or almond extract.

MIX until dry ingredients are coated.

BAKE at 350° for 20 to 25 minutes, STIRRING often to brown evenly.

COOL. STIR until crumbly.

STORE in tightly covered container.

Note: If you omit sugar, increase honey to 1 cup.

This looks great in a champagne glass!

STRAWBERRY BREAKFAST

LAYER sweetened berries with granola and plain yogurt.

"As long as you're home, you'll eat a good breakfast!" my mother used to say. To speed up the porridge in the morning . . .

OATMEAL MIX

8 cups uncooked quick oats	2 teaspoons salt
1/2 cup packed brown sugar	2 1/2 teaspoons cinnamon
	1 1/2 teaspoons nutmeg
	1 1/2 cups raisins or dried fruit

COMBINE all ingredients in large bowl.

STORE in tightly sealed 10-cup container.

USE within 6 months.

OATMEAL PORRIDGE

1/2 cup oatmeal mix (see recipe above)
1/2 cup boiling water

ADD oatmeal mix to boiling water in small saucepan.

STIR and SIMMER over medium heat 1 to 2 minutes.

Yield: 1 serving

Sauces

*THE FACT IS THAT IT TAKES MORE THAN
INGREDIENTS AND TECHNIQUE TO COOK
A GOOD MEAL. A GOOD COOK PUTS
SOMETHING OF HIMSELF INTO THE
PREPARATION—HE COOKS WITH ENJOYMENT,
ANTICIPATION, SPONTANEITY, AND HE IS
WILLING TO EXPERIMENT.*

—Pearl Bailey
  (from *Bartlett's Quotations*)

You might assume that a sauce would be wheat-free, but one look at the label could surprise you. If you must avoid distilled vinegar, try this recipe from Jeanne Huffstutter of Portland, Ore.

JUST KETCHUP

8 ounces tomato sauce
6 ounces tomato paste
2 ounces water
1/3 cup cider vinegar
  (see note)
1/4 tablespoon allspice

1/2 cinnamon stick
1/8 teaspoon cloves
3/8 teaspoon paprika
1/2 teaspoon dry mustard
Dash cayenne pepper

COMBINE all ingredients in saucepan.

SIMMER, STIRRING to prevent sticking, until thick, about 45 minutes

OR

MICROWAVE on high 4 minutes, turning once.

MICROWAVE on medium-low 10 minutes.

REMOVE cinnamon stick and COOL.

KEEP refrigerated.

Note: Substituting wine or rice vinegar works well, also.

Yield: approximately 20 ounces (2 1/2 cups)

BARBEQUE SAUCE

1 cup ketchup (see recipe above)
1/3 cup Worcestershire
   sauce
1 teaspoon chili powder

1 teaspoon salt
1 teaspoon brown sugar
1 cup water

HEAT all ingredients in saucepan until well mixed.

STORE in jar in refrigerator.

BAR B QUE SAUCE PROVENCALE

1 8-ounce can tomato sauce
2 tablespoons frozen orange
   juice concentrate, thawed
1 tablespoon water
2 teaspoons garlic powder

1 1/2 teaspoons tarragon,
   crushed
1/4 teaspoon pepper
1 tablespoon onion powder

BRING all ingredients to a boil in saucepan, STIRRING occasionally.

STORE in jar in refrigerator.

Tamari is wheat-free soy sauce, so this is safe.

TERIYAKI SAUCE

1 cup Mirin (Japanese sweet cooking wine)
1 cup tamari
1 or 2 slices fresh ginger
1 or 2 cloves garlic, minced

HEAT wine to boiling in saucepan and COOK a few minutes to remove alcohol.

ADD tamari, ginger, and garlic. COOK a few minutes longer.

Yield: 1 1/2 cups

This sauce goes well with fish, especially salmon.

CUCUMBER SAUCE

1 cucumber, peeled and quartered lengthwise
Salt and pepper
1 cup yogurt or sour cream
1 teaspoon grated lemon rind
1/2 teaspoon lemon juice
Dill

SLICE cucumber thinly. SPRINKLE with salt.

SET ASIDE 15 minutes, then DRAIN.

ADD remaining ingredients and MIX well.

Yield: 2 cups

ORANGE SAUCE FOR CHICKEN OR STIR-FRY

2 tablespoons tamari
6 tablespoons water
2 tablespoons dry sherry
2 tablespoons orange
*   marmalade*

2 teaspoons cornstarch
2 teaspoons minced ginger
1/2 teaspoon cayenne pepper
*   (optional)*

COMBINE all ingredients in saucepan and HEAT thoroughly.
STORE in jar in refrigerator. Keeps several weeks.

ORANGE SAUCE 2

(for rice or poultry)
   1 10 to 12-ounce can chicken bouillon or broth
   1 10 to 12-ounce can frozen orange juice concentrate

COMBINE all ingredients in saucepan.
HEAT and serve.
STORE in jar in refrigerator. Keeps several weeks.

ORANGE SAUCE 3

1 cup granulated sugar
1/4 teaspoon salt
2 tablespoons cornstarch

1 cup orange juice
3/4 cup water
1/4 cup lemon juice

COMBINE all ingredients in saucepan.

BRING to a boil and LET COOL.

STORE in jar in refrigerator. Keeps several weeks.

TACO SAUCE

1 14-ounce can
   (1 1/2 cups) tomatoes
1 8-ounce can tomato sauce
2 teaspoons chili powder
1/2 cup chopped onion

1/4 teaspoon cayenne pepper
1 teaspoon salt
1/2 teaspoon celery salt
Few drops hot pepper sauce

COMBINE all ingredients in saucepan.

COOK 10 minutes.

STORE in refrigerator.

RED CHILI SAUCE

1/3 cup shortening	*1 teaspoon garlic powder or*
1/2 cup bean flour	*2 cloves minced garlic*
2 to 3 tablespoons chili powder	*1/2 teaspoon salt*
2 cups tomato juice	*Pinch cumin*
2 cups water	*Pinch oregano*

HEAT shortening in large saucepan and STIR in flour and
chili powder.

SAUTE until color starts to turn brown—this develops the flavor.

STIR in remaining ingredients until mixture thickens.

SIMMER 15 to 20 minutes.

SERVE with enchiladas.

GREEN CHILI SAUCE

3 cups chicken stock
1/2 cup chopped onion
1 large tomato (fresh
   or canned), chopped
1 4-ounce can diced green
   peeled chilis

1/2 teaspoon garlic powder
1/2 teaspoon salt
1/8 teaspoon pepper
1/2 cup bean flour
1 cup water

COMBINE all ingredients except flour and water in large saucepan.
BRING to a boil. SIMMER 15 minutes.

MAKE a paste of flour and water and STIR into cooking sauce to thicken.

MEXICALI MEAT SAUCE

1 tablespoon olive or
   vegetable oil
1 tablespoon chili powder
1 tablespoon flour
3 cups water

1/2 onion, chopped
2 cloves garlic, minced
1/2 teaspoon cumin
Sliced onions, peppers, etc.

MIX oil, chili powder, and flour into a paste in medium saucepan.

ADD water and BRING to a boil. BOIL 3 minutes.

ADD chopped onion, garlic, and cumin.

ADD sliced onions, peppers, etc.

USE with cooked beef or chicken for fajitas. Also good in tacos, taco salad, enchiladas.

CHILI SAUCE MIX

3 tablespoons rice flour
1/2 cup instant minced onion
2 tablespoons chili powder
1 tablespoon salt
1/2 teaspoon cayenne
  pepper

2 teaspoons instant minced
  garlic
2 teaspoons granulated sugar
2 teaspoons cumin

COMBINE all ingredients and MIX well.

ADJUST seasonings to taste by varying pepper and chili powder.

STORE in labeled glass jar.

WINTER NIGHT CHILI

1 pound lean ground beef
2 16-ounce cans kidney
  beans
2 16-ounce cans
  tomatoes

1/4 cup Chili Sauce Mix
  (see recipe above)

BROWN beef in a large skillet and DRAIN.

ADD remaining ingredients.

SIMMER 15 minutes, STIRRING occasionally.

Yield: 4 to 6 servings

HORSERADISH SAUCE

2 cups horseradish
1/2 pint sour cream, dairy
  or non-dairy
1/2 cup wine or cider vinegar
2 tablespoons granulated sugar

PEEL and grate horseradish or PROCESS small chunks in processor.
FOLD in sour cream and vinegar to desired consistency.
PACK in small sterile baby food jars.
TOP with sugar to keep horseradish from darkening.
REFRIGERATE.

Great brushed on a baked ham or . . .

HAM GLAZE

1 cup light or dark corn
  syrup
1/2 cup packed brown
  sugar

3 tablespoons prepared
  mustard
1/2 teaspoon ginger

BRING corn syrup, brown sugar, mustard, and ginger to a boil in
small saucepan and BOIL 5 minutes.
STORE in labeled jar in refrigerator.

Yield: 1 cup

ORANGE TURKEY GLAZE

1 cup light corn syrup
1 cup orange juice
1/4 cup grated orange rind

COMBINE all ingredients in bowl and MIX well.
STORE in labeled jar in refrigerator.

Yield: 2 1/4 cups

Brush frequently on turkey the last 30 minutes of baking.

Great with poultry . . .

PLUM SAUCE

2/3 cup plum butter (see note)
4 teaspoons orange juice
2 teaspoons red wine vinegar
*1/8 teaspoon grated orange
    rind*

1/4 teaspoon dry mustard
1/8 teaspoon tamari
Pinch cardamom

COMBINE all ingredients and COOK over low heat, STIRRING
until mixture is smooth.
STORE in labeled jar in refrigerator.

Yield: 1 cup

Note: You can find plum butter with the jams in your supermarket.

This is so good with turkey, chicken, and pork.

PLUM SAUCE 2

1 1-pound can whole
  purple plums
2 tablespoons butter or
  margarine
1 medium onion, chopped
1/4 cup packed brown sugar

1/4 cup tomato chili
  sauce (see note)
2 tablespoons tamari
1 teaspoon ginger
2 teaspoons lemon juice

DRAIN plums, RESERVING 2 tablespoons syrup. REMOVE pits.

PUREE plums and reserved syrup and SET ASIDE.

PLACE butter in 1-quart microwavable dish.

COVER with wax paper or loose plastic wrap and MICROWAVE on high 20 seconds.

ADD onion and MICROWAVE on high 2 minutes.

STIR in remaining ingredients.

MICROWAVE on high 3 minutes or until sauce thickens slightly.

PASS sauce at the table.

KEEPS well in refrigerator. STORE in labeled jar.

Note: You can find tomato chili sauce with the ketchup in your supermarket.

MAYONNAISE

1 whole egg or 3 egg yolks (see note)
1 teaspoon prepared mustard
1 tablespoon wine vinegar or lemon juice
1 cup vegetable oil
Salt and pepper

PROCESS egg or egg yolks, mustard, and vinegar or lemon juice in
blender or processor 3 seconds.

With processor still running, ADD oil a few drops at a time. PUT lip
of measuring cup over side of processing bowl and POUR very slowly.
Mayonnaise will thicken.

TASTE and SEASON with a few more drops vinegar, salt, and
pepper, if desired.

Yield: 1 cup

Note: Whole egg mayonnaise is softer than mayonnaise made with
only the yolks.

Mixes well with tuna.

EGG-FREE MAYONNAISE

1/4 cup wine or
  cider vinegar
3/4 cup olive oil
1 teaspoon salt
1 teaspoon granulated
  sugar or honey

1 teaspoon Dijon-style
  Mustard (see p. 308)
1 cup mashed potatoes,
  preferably hot (see note)
Pinch of herbs (optional)

COMBINE all ingredients except potatoes and herbs, if using.

PROCESS in blender or food processor, until smooth.

ADD enough potatoes to thicken.

ADD favorite herbs, if using, such as parsley, dill, or basil.

COOL. Mayonnaise thickens as it cools.

STORE in labeled jar in refrigerator.

Note: Try substituting 1 cup tofu.

Wonderful poured over cooked fish, especially catfish!

PECAN BUTTER SAUCE

1/2 cup finely chopped pecans
1/4 cup butter or margarine
1 tablespoon lemon juice
1 teaspoon Worcestershire sauce

COMBINE all ingredients in a small saucepan and HEAT thoroughly.

Yield: 1/2 cup

Mustard is a fun food to make. It will never go bad.
It may dry out and lose its flavor, but it will not harm you.

SPICY MUSTARD

(You will need additional time.)

1/3 cup light mustard seeds	*1/2 teaspoon cinnamon*
1/4 cup (1 ounce) dry mustard	*1/4 teaspoon allspice*
1/2 cup cold water	*1/4 teaspoon dill seeds*
1 cup cider vinegar	*1/4 teaspoon dried tarragon*
2 tablespoons brown sugar	*1/8 teaspoon turmeric*
1 teaspoon salt	*1 to 2 tablespoons honey*
2 cloves garlic, minced	

SOAK mustard seeds and dry mustard in cold water 3 hours.

COMBINE vinegar, sugar, salt, garlic, cinnamon, allspice, dill, tarragon, and turmeric in 1-quart non-corroding pan (AVOID aluminum).

SIMMER over medium heat about 15 minutes, until liquid is reduced by half.

POUR liquid through strainer into mustard mixture.

PUREE in blender or processor.

COOK in top of double boiler until thickened, 10 to 15 minutes. Mixture will thicken more as it cools.

STIR in honey.

COOL and PACK into a jar, COVERING tightly.

STORE in refrigerator at least 1 week before using.

It will keep up to 2 years.

Use this mustard to hold together the oil and vinegar in salad dressings. It's also good with a grilled cheese sandwich.

This delightful mustard recipe is reprinted with permission from Helene Sawyer, author of Gourmet Mustards: How to Make and Cook with Them *(Culinary Arts Ltd., Lake Oswego, Ore.).*

BASIC DIJON-STYLE MUSTARD

2 cups dry white wine
1 large onion, chopped
3 cloves garlic, pressed
1 cup (4 ounces)
  dry mustard

3 tablespoons honey
1 tablespoon oil
2 teaspoons salt

COMBINE wine, onion, and garlic in a large saucepan.

HEAT to boiling and SIMMER 5 minutes.

COOL and DISCARD strained solids.

ADD this liquid to dry mustard, STIRRING constantly until smooth.

BLEND in honey, oil, and salt.

RETURN to saucepan (have hankies ready or hold face away from steam).

HEAT slowly until thickened, STIRRING constantly.

COOL, then PLACE in covered jar.

AGE in cool, dark place 2 to 8 weeks, depending upon pungency desired.

STORE in refrigerator.

You can be creative here, adding honey or herbs or using wine or rice or apple cider vinegar, but not grain vinegar, and blending well with the basic recipe.

This is an excellent substitute for your regular spaghetti sauce.

PESTO SAUCE

1 ounce Parmesan cheese
1/4 cup walnuts
1 cup fresh basil
   leaves (see note)
1/3 cup olive oil

2 to 3 cloves garlic,
   pressed
1/2 teaspoon salt
Black pepper to taste

GRATE cheese in food processor.

MEASURE 1/4 cup cheese into mixing bowl.

PROCESS nuts briefly to chop them. ADD to cheese.

PROCESS basil leaves and oil until nearly smooth.

COMBINE with cheese mixture and ADD remaining ingredients.

ADD extra oil if mix is not runny.

POUR into 1-cup jar, CLEANING pesto from sides.

POUR a little olive oil over top and STORE in refrigerator.

Note: Or use 1 cup firmly packed parsley plus 1 tablespoon dried sweet basil.

Use over corn or rice pasta, with fresh tomatoes, shrimp, peas, and a little lemon juice. Pour olive oil over top of pesto each time you use it. Keeps about 1 year refrigerated.

SAUCES WITH TOMATOES

When cooking with tomatoes, whether making sauces or gazpacho, add a piece of carrot. It will cut the acidic taste, making a sweeter product.

Great for fish, especially salmon or steelhead . . .

TOMATO HERB SAUCE

1 8-ounce can tomato sauce	1 teaspoon lemon juice
1/4 cup water or white wine	1/2 teaspoon dried basil
(sauterne or chablis)	1/2 teaspoon dried thyme
2 tablespoons oil or butter	

COMBINE all ingredients in saucepan.

BRING to a boil and SIMMER 5 minutes.

PLACE fish in shallow baking pan.

POUR sauce over fish.

Bake at 350° for 30 minutes.

Yield: covers 6 servings of fish

Good over spaghetti or rice or . . .

ITALIAN SAUCE

3 tablespoons oil
1 onion, chopped
1 clove garlic, minced
1 green pepper, chopped
1 cup sliced mushrooms
3 tablespoons rice flour
1 1-pound can whole
tomatoes

1/4 teaspoon oregano
1 teaspoon salt
1 pound ground beef,
browned (optional)
1/2 cup red table wine
Spaghetti or rice, cooked

HEAT oil in skillet and SAUTE onion, garlic, pepper, and mushrooms.

STIR in flour.

ADD tomatoes, oregano, and salt, and STIR until thickened. ADD beef, if using.

ADD wine and SERVE over corn spaghetti, rice, or biscuits.

Yield: 4 to 6 servings

WHEAT-FREE WHITE SAUCE MIX

2 cups non-fat
  milk powder or
  non-dairy creamer
3/4 cup cornstarch
1/4 cup chicken bouillon
  powder

4 teaspoons onion powder
1 teaspoon dried thyme
1 teaspoon dried basil
1/2 teaspoon freshly
  ground pepper

COMBINE all ingredients.
STORE in tightly sealed container.

WHEAT-FREE WHITE SAUCE

1/4 cup Wheat-Free White Sauce Mix (see recipe above)
1 cup water or milk

COMBINE mix and water or milk in saucepan.
STIR until smooth.
ADD 1 tablespoon butter.
HEAT and STIR until thickened.

So good over ice cream or French toast.

BLUEBERRY SAUCE

1 cup fresh or frozen blueberries
1/2 cup water
1 cup granulated sugar

1 tablespoon lemon juice
1 tablespoon butter
(optional)

COMBINE all ingredients except butter in large saucepan.

SIMMER 10 to 15 minutes or until slightly thickened.

REMOVE from heat.

ADD butter, if using.

STIR and COOL slightly.

ADD 1 cup of fresh blueberries, if desired, before serving.

This recipe makes it easy to have a safe salad dressing handy.

FRENCH DRESSING MIX

1 cup granulated sugar
2 tablespoons paprika
4 teaspoons dry mustard
2 tablespoons salt
1/2 teaspoon onion powder

COMBINE all ingredients in mixing bowl and MIX well.
STORE in a labeled glass jar.

TO MIX UP A BATCH . . .

5 tablespoons French Dressing Mix (see recipe above)
3/4 cup olive or canola oil
1/4 cup cider or wine vinegar

COMBINE all ingredients in jar.
SHAKE before using.
STORE in refrigerator.

SALAD DRESSINGS WITH LESS FAT, MORE FLAVOR

- SUBSTITUTE a darker, more flavorful oil, such as sesame oil, for the oil in your recipe and CUT the amount by as much as half.
- SUBSTITUTE a more flavorful vinegar, such as rice vinegar or a fruity vinegar, and CUT down on oil. Or USE just vinegar.
- MAKE your own more flavorful vinegar by STEEPING an herb in good white wine vinegar or cider vinegar. USE just the vinegar on salad.
- Just a reminder: If you need to avoid all grains, do not use white distilled vinegar, which is made from grains.

SIMPLE, SWEET SALAD DRESSING

1/3 cup wine vinegar
1 teaspoon onion powder
1 teaspoon honey
2/3 cup canola oil

2 tablespoons water
1 tablespoon
  crumbled bacon

COMBINE all ingredients in a jar and SHAKE.

STORE in refrigerator.

Excellent with fruit salads. (I like it with grapefruit.)

*If you must avoid mayonnaise, you will enjoy this dressing for
cole slaw, potato salad, or wheat-free pasta salads.*

BOILED SALAD DRESSING

1 teaspoon dry mustard	*1 tablespoon granulated sugar*
1 teaspoon salt	*1/3 cup wine or cider vinegar*
1 teaspoon cornstarch or	*1 egg yolk*
arrowroot flour	*1 tablespoon water*

BLEND in bowl or blender all ingredients until smooth.

POUR into heavy saucepan or skillet.

COOK over medium heat until thickened, STIRRING constantly.

COOK 1 minute more.

COOL. STORE in refrigerator.

BASIC SALAD DRESSING

1 teaspoon salt	*2/3 cup oil*
1/8 teaspoon pepper	*1 teaspoon xanthan gum*
1 teaspoon dry mustard	*(optional)*
1/4 cup cider or wine vinegar	

COMBINE all ingredients in a jar and MIX well.

STORE in refrigerator.

Different oils give a different taste, so be adventurous! Also, try
adding anchovies, garlic, parsley, onions, etc.

SEAFOOD SALAD DRESSING

8 *sprigs watercress*	*Boiling water*
6 *spinach or chard leaves*	1 *cup mayonnaise*
5 *sprigs parsley*	2 *teaspoons lemon juice*

PUT watercress, spinach or chard leaves, and parsley in bowl and COVER with boiling water.

LET STAND 5 minutes.

DRAIN and RINSE twice in cold water.

ADD to processor with mayonnaise.

ADD lemon juice.

PROCESS until blended.

STORE in refrigerator.

Yield: 2 to 3 cups

Good for salad dressing or sandwich spread . . .

GUACAMOLE

1 large avocado	*Dash garlic salt*
1/8 teaspoon salt	*Dash hot sauce*

MASH avocado in medium bowl.

ADD remaining ingredients and MIX well.

STORE in covered container in refrigerator.

CLAM SAUCE

2 6 1/2-ounce cans	*1 clove garlic, minced*
chopped clams	*1 tablespoon dried parsley*
1 cup water	*Salt to taste*
2 tablespoons olive oil	

COMBINE all ingredients in saucepan.

HEAT and SERVE.

Spreads

WE CANNOT TELL THE PRECISE MOMENT WHEN FRIENDSHIP IS FORMED. AS IN FILLING A VESSEL DROP BY DROP, THERE IS AT LAST A DROP WHICH MAKES IT RUN OVER: SO IN A SERIES OF KINDNESSES THERE IS AT LAST ONE WHICH MAKES THE HEART RUN OVER.

—James Boswell, 1777

NUT AND RAISIN SPREAD

1 medium orange
1 cup broken pecans
2 1/2 cups light raisins, divided
3/4 cup mayonnaise or salad dressing
Orange slices, celery sticks, or crackers

QUARTER and seed orange, but do not peel.

PROCESS orange and nuts until finely chopped.

ADD 1 1/4 cups raisins and mayonnaise or salad dressing.

PROCESS until raisins are chopped.

ADD remaining raisins and PROCESS until finely chopped.

SPREAD on orange slices, celery, or crackers.

STORE in covered container in refrigerator

OR

FREEZE up to 3 months. THAW in refrigerator.

Yield: 3 1/2 cups

SPINACH DIP

1 10- or 12-ounce box frozen
   chopped spinach
4 green onions
3/4 cup parsley sprigs
1 cup mayonnaise

1 tablespoon lemon juice
1/4 teaspoon salt
1/8 teaspoon nutmeg
Dash cayenne pepper

COOK and DRAIN spinach.

COOL and SET ASIDE.

CUT onions in 1-inch lengths.

PROCESS onions with parsley until finely chopped.

ADD mayonnaise, lemon juice, salt, nutmeg, and pepper.

PROCESS until blended.

DRAIN spinach again and ADD to mixture.

PROCESS just enough to blend (2 on-off bursts). Do not puree.

COVER and CHILL.

Yield: 2 cups

Lots of good calcium here . . .

CLAM DIP

6 ounces cream cheese
1 teaspoon salt
1/2 teaspoon hot pepper sauce
1 tablespoon grated onion
1 7 1/2-ounce can clam pieces,
    drained, reserving 2 teaspoons
    juice

1 cup sour cream
Sliced olives

SOFTEN cream cheese at room temperature.

BLEND in salt, hot sauce, and onion.

ADD clams and reserved clam juice.

STIR in sour cream.

CHILL covered at least 1/2 hour before serving.

GARNISH with sliced olives.

Yield: 2 cups

SERVE as dip for crackers, chips, or raw vegetables.

Another good source of calcium . . .

SALMON DIP

1 8-ounce package cream cheese
1 tablespoon prepared mustard
1 tablespoon wine or cider vinegar
2 tablespoons grated onion
1 teaspoon Worcestershire sauce
1/3 cup light cream
1 7 3/4-ounce can salmon

SOFTEN cream cheese at room temperature.

BLEND with remaining ingredients except salmon.

FLAKE salmon and ADD to cream cheese.

BEAT until well blended.

COVER and CHILL several hours to blend flavors.

Yield: 2 cups

SERVE with crackers or chips.

SHRIMP DIP

1 7-ounce can small shrimp
1 8-ounce package cream
  cheese (see note)
1 to 2 tablespoons grated onion

2 to 3 tablespoons parsley
Several drops hot pepper sauce
Mayonnaise for thinning

MIX all ingredients in a bowl. COVER and CHILL.

Note: Or substitute non-dairy sour cream or tofu.

LIVER PATÉ

1/2 pound liverwurst
1 3-ounce package cream
  cheese (see note)
2 tablespoons mayonnaise
2 tablespoons cream

2 teaspoons
  Worcestershire sauce
1 tablespoon Sherry
1 teaspoon seasoned salt

MIX all ingredients in a bowl. COVER and CHILL.

Note: Or substitute non-dairy sour cream or tofu.

Beverages

*THE FINEST GIFT WE CAN GIVE
TO OUR AGE AND TIME IS THE
GIFT OF A CONSTRUCTIVE AND
CREATIVE LIFE.*

—Unknown

*THAT WHICH THE FOUNTAIN SENDS FORTH
RETURNS AGAIN TO THE FOUNTAIN.*

—Henry Wadsworth Longfellow

The buttermilk and sherbet combination is what makes this drink.

ENERGY FLIP

1/2 banana
1 scoop sherbet

1 cup buttermilk
1 tablespoon protein powder

COMBINE all ingredients in blender and MIX until smooth.

Yield: 1 serving

ORANGE BLUSH

1 cup fresh strawberries
4 cups orange juice
3 ice cubes

COMBINE all ingredients in blender and MIX until smooth.

Yield: 2 servings

PINK SUNRISE

1 cup fresh strawberries
3 cups pink grapefruit juice
1 banana

COMBINE all ingredients in blender and MIX until smooth.

Yield: 2 servings

These little tidbits are so easy and so good!

SUPER FRUIT SHAKE

6 large ripe strawberries
1 large banana
1 5 1/2-ounce can apricot
   or peach nectar

1 teaspoon honey
3 ice cubes

COMBINE all ingredients in blender and MIX until smooth.

Yield: 1 serving

Ginger is soothing to the digestive tract.

GINGER TEA

10 thin slices ginger root
3 cups good well water
1 teaspoon anise or fennel seeds

SIMMER ginger root in water 15 minutes.
ADD anise or fennel seeds to make tea naturally sweet.
STRAIN and ENJOY.

Never a risk of corn syrup or preservatives
when you make your own . . .

GRAPE JUICE

2 cups grapes	*Water*
1 cup sugar	

FILL 1-quart jar with grapes and sugar.

ADD water, but allow 1/2-inch head space.

SCREW lid on tightly.

PUT jar in canner and COVER with water.

BRING to a boil and BOIL 10 minutes.

TURN off heat and LET STAND until cold.

Yield: 1 quart

Dilute with cold water if desired when serving.

BRANDIED CIDER

1 quart cider	*1 whole nutmeg*
3 tablespoons honey	*1 2-inch cinnamon stick*
2 tablespoons lemon juice	*1/4 to 1/3 cup brandy*
4 whole cloves	

COMBINE cider, honey, and lemon in saucepan.

PLACE spices in double thickness cheesecloth and TIE.

ADD cheesecloth bag to cider mixture.

COVER and HEAT but don't boil.

STIR in brandy and SERVE immediately.

Yield: 6 servings

*Many Scandinavian countries have something similar to
this little German holiday beverage.*

GLUHWEIN

1 bottle claret	*1 1-inch cinnamon stick*
6 teaspoons granulated sugar	*3 strips orange peel*
3 whole cloves	*3 strips lemon peel*

HEAT all ingredients in saucepan, but don't boil.

STRAIN into pitcher.

THRUST in a hot poker—if you want to be traditional—and

SERVE.

KAHLUA

(You will need additional time.)

2 ounces instant coffee
  (see note)
2 cups boiling water
3 1/2 cups granulated
  sugar

1 vanilla bean cut into 4 pieces
1 quart brandy
1 pint vodka (see note)

ADD coffee to water slowly, MIXING well.

COOL.

PLACE vanilla bean pieces in 2 1/2-quart jar.

ADD cooled coffee mixture.

ADD brandy and vodka and MIX.

COVER tightly and LET STAND 30 days.

REMOVE vanilla bean pieces.

TRANSFER to small sterilized bottles and STORE.

Yield: 2 1/2 quarts

Note: Yes, Emily, my friend, it has to be instant coffee. Regular just won't do it!

Note: Vodka should be distilled from grapes or potatoes, not grains.

Miscellaneous

WHAT IS SUCCESS?

TO LAUGH OFTEN AND MUCH;
TO WIN THE RESPECT OF INTELLIGENT PEOPLE
*   AND THE AFFECTION OF CHILDREN;*
TO EARN THE APPRECIATION OF HONEST CRITICS AND
*   ENDURE THE BETRAYAL OF FALSE FRIENDS;*
TO APPRECIATE BEAUTY;
TO FIND THE BEST IN OTHERS;
TO LEAVE THE WORLD A BIT BETTER, WHETHER BY
*   A HEALTHY CHILD, A GARDEN PATCH*
*   OR A REDEEMED SOCIAL CONDITION;*
TO KNOW EVEN ONE LIFE HAS BREATHED
*   EASIER BECAUSE YOU HAVE LIVED;*
THIS IS TO HAVE SUCCEEDED.

—Ralph Waldo Emerson

HOMEMADE APPLE PECTIN

(You will need additional time.)
8 medium, tart, slightly underripe apples (see note)
4 cups water
2 tablespoons lemon juice

WASH apples and CUT into small pieces without peeling.

REMOVE stems and blossom ends.

PUT apples in large pot and barely COVER with water.

COVER and COOK slowly about 40 minutes or until fruit is soft.

POUR cooked fruit into dampened jelly bag (see note).

LET hang over a bowl overnight to EXTRACT as much juice as possible without squeezing.

STERILIZE 6 to 8 small canning jars and lids by boiling 3 minutes.

BOIL juice rapidly 15 minutes.

POUR boiling juice into sterilized jars and SEAL.

PROCESS 5 minutes in boiling water bath or KEEP refrigerated.

To use this process with red currants, mash them before letting them drip.

Note: Don't use overripe fruit when making jams and jellies because it has little pectin and often gives runny results. In fact, slightly underripe fruit has the highest pectin content. Also, pectin is concentrated in the skin and core of the fruit, so do not peel or core it.

Note: You can purchase a cloth bag from a kitchenware or department store to serve as a jelly bag.

*A way of flavoring soup or stew without the mess of fishing out
herb sprigs before serving . . .*

BOUQUETS GARNIS

Sprigs of thyme	OR
1 bay leaf	*1 stalk celery*
2 or 3 fresh parsley sprigs	*1 sprig lovage, marjoram,*
	or savory
	Peel of 1 orange

TIE herb sprigs in a bundle with string and PLACE in pot.
REMOVE bundle at the end of cooking time.

*"Gorp" has been a traditional trail mix or snack
for our family's outings.*

GORP

1 cup raisins	*1/2 cup almonds or cashews*
1 cup soy nuts or peanuts	*1/2 cup M&M's or*
1/2 cup coconut	*chocolate chips*

MIX all ingredients. STORE in air-tight container.

ROASTING NUTS

Hazelnuts or Filberts

SPREAD shelled nuts in shallow pan.

ROAST at 275° for 20 to 30 minutes.

WRAP nuts in a dish towel and steam 1 minute.

RUB nuts in towel to REMOVE skins.

STORE in refrigerator or freezer.

Walnuts

SPREAD shelled halves or pieces in shallow pan.

ROAST at 350° for 15 minutes.

STORE in airtight container in refrigerator or freezer.

Almonds

SPREAD shelled nuts in shallow pan.

ROAST at 325° about 15 to 20 minutes.

STIR often.

STORE in airtight container in refrigerator or freezer.

Note: You preserve nutrients by always roasting before chopping.

CANNING FRUITS AND NUTS

Dried Fruits and Nuts

STERILIZE jars in preheated oven at 150° for 20 minutes.

FILL sterilized jars with dried fruits, nuts, grains, or pasta.

PLACE on shallow pan in oven and BAKE at 150 to 175° for 30 to 40 minutes.

REMOVE from oven and COOL.

Fruits without Granulated Sugar

STERILIZE jars in pre-heated oven at 150° for 20 minutes.

POUR 1 to 2 cups boiling water into each jar.

ADD 1 large spoonful honey.

DROP in 1 1/2 cups fruit.

ADD boiling water to top and SEAL.

Pick flowers from your (or a friend's) garden and find the other ingredients at your health food store or drugstore.

CALENDULA CREAM

(You will need additional time.)
   3 or 4 calendula flowers (see note)
   1 cup olive oil
   1/2 ounce or more beeswax (see note)

CHOP calendula flowers. PUT in 10-ounce clear glass jar.
COVER with olive oil and PUT lid on.
PLACE in sun and LET SIT about 2 weeks (longer if season or weather is not very sunny).

To mix up a batch:
STERILIZE small glass jars and lids by boiling 3 minutes.
STRAIN flower mixture through clean cotton cloth.
POUR remaining liquid in sterile glass jar.
HEAT in double boiler or electric skillet with 1 inch water.
ADD beeswax in small pieces (see note). STIR until dissolved.
POUR hot mixture carefully into jars and LABEL.
Yes, labeling is important even if you think you have a good memory. Someone might accidentally moisturize the inside of a stomach!
STORE in refrigerator.
This cream will keep outside the refrigerator if you are careful to use an applicator and not your fingers, which are more likely to introduce mold.

Note: If you are sensitive to foods you may also be sensitive to chemicals in cosmetics. Calendula is a lovely flower that has proved to be kind to the skin and makes a more than satisfactory skin moisturizer. You will feel the difference. Make only a little at first just to be sure you are not sensitive to these ingredients.

Note: The amount of beeswax used determines heaviness; 1/2 ounce makes an easily spreadable cream.

Fresh flowers will last longer in a vase with this recipe.

FRESH FLOWER SAVER

1 quart water
1 tablespoon granulated sugar

2 tablespoons lime
 or lemon juice
1/2 teaspoon liquid bleach

MIX ingredients and pour into your vase.

A completely natural potpourri can be more tolerable to those of us with sensitive noses.

POTPOURRI

Peel of 1 grapefruit
 (see note)
Peel of 2 oranges
Peel of 2 lemons

4 cups water
2 cinnamon sticks
1 tablespoon cloves
1 tablespoon allspice

COMBINE all ingredients in medium saucepan and BRING to boil.
SIMMER to provide fragrance throughout your house.
REFRIGERATE between simmerings.
Note: Use a potato peeler to obtain the zest, or citrus peel, and you will not lose the oils in the skin. Save peels in a sealed bag in the freezer.

Good as a night cream or for chapped hands. Borax is a skin softener; zinc heals irritated skin.

ALMOND CREAM

1 ounce beeswax
1 teaspoon anhydrous lanolin
5 ounces almond oil, divided
1 teaspoon zinc oxide

1/2 teaspoon borax dissolved
* in 2 ounces bottled or*
* boiled water*
1 drop scented oil (optional)

STERILIZE small glass jars and lids by boiling 3 minutes.

SET UP double boiler or SET small pyrex container in water in a skillet (called a water bath).

BREAK beeswax into little pieces so it melts easier.

COMBINE beeswax and lanolin and HEAT in water bath just until beeswax is melted. Do not let wax simmer.

CAUTION: Don't heat wax with small children around or become distracted and leave it. You must watch it carefully.

REMOVE from heat and slowly ADD 3 ounces almond oil.

MIX in a separate dish zinc oxide and 2 ounces almond oil until smooth.

ADD zinc mixture to beeswax, BEATING continuously.

ADD borax mixture to beeswax and BEAT until cool.

ADD scented oil, if using.

Yes, labeling is important even if you think you have a good memory. Someone might accidentally moisturize the inside of a stomach!

STORE in refrigerator.

This cream will keep outside the refrigerator if you are careful to use an applicator and not your fingers, which are more likely to introduce mold.

Conversion Table

IF YOU WANT HAPPINESS FOR AN HOUR—
TAKE A NAP.
IF YOU WANT HAPPINESS FOR A DAY—
GO FISHING.
IF YOU WANT HAPPINESS FOR A MONTH—
GET MARRIED.
IF YOU WANT HAPPINESS FOR A YEAR—
INHERIT A FORTUNE.
IF YOU WANT HAPPINESS FOR A LIFETIME—
HELP SOMEONE ELSE.

—Chinese proverb

CONVERSION TABLE FOR U.S. TO METRIC COOKING

Liquid and Dry Measures

U.S.	Metric
1/4 teaspoon	1.25 milliliters
1/2 teaspoon	2.5 milliliters
1 teaspoon	5 milliliters
1 tablespoon (3 teaspoons)	15 milliliters
1 fluid ounce (2 tablespoons)	30 milliliters
1/4 cup	60 milliliters
1/3 cup	80 milliliters
1 cup	240 milliliters
1 pint (2 cups)	480 milliliters
1 quart (4 cups)	960 milliliters
1 gallon (4 quarts)	3.8 liters

Weight Measures

U.S.	Metric
1 ounce	28 grams
1 pound	454 grams

Oven Temperatures

Fahrenheit degrees	Celsius degrees	Gas mark
250	120	1/2
275	140	1
300	150	2
325	160	3
350	180	4
375	190	5
400	200	6
425	220	7
450	230	8
475	240	9
500	260	10

INDEX

MY OWN RECIPES

MY OWN RECIPES

MY OWN RECIPES

Beyond Words Publishing, Inc.

Our corporate mission:
Inspire to Integrity

Our declared values:
We give to all of life as life has given us.
We honor all relationships.
Trust and stewardship are integral to fulfilling dreams.
Collaboration is essential to create miracles.
Creativity and aesthetics nourish the soul.
Unlimited thinking is fundamental.
Living your passion is vital.
Joy and humor open our hearts to growth.
It is important to remind ourselves of love.